More Praise for *Kick-Start Your Class*

"This book is a treasure for all professionals—teachers, coaches, administrators—who work with groups and want to set up their time together for success. *Kick-Start Your Class* is chock full of pragmatic activities to start your classes with both brains and heart. And they're easy to read and follow! My copy will be a well-worn fixture in my classes and workshops."
—Dawn Wink, author of *Teaching Passionately: What's Love Got To Do With It?*

"An amazing gift for a student or a beginning or seasoned teacher, LouAnne Johnson's *Kick Start Your Class: Academic Icebreakers to Engage Students* offers a rich compilation of multi-disciplinary, ready-to-teach classroom starters, concept-builders, and closers that will invigorate the culture and climate of any classroom. This is not a book that will sit on a teacher's shelf; reaching for this set of lesson gems will quickly become second nature to creative teachers."
—Pamela Prosise, thirty-year veteran teacher and literacy specialist, McMinnville School District, McMinnville, Oregon

"LouAnne Johnson's book on student engagement is packed with priceless lessons and activities for today's teachers. It doesn't matter whether you work in a regular day class or an after school setting; or whether you're a first-year intern, an instructional leader, or a life-long teacher, *Kick-Start Your Class* is a must-have resource for all educators."
—Jim Vidak, Tulare County Superintendent of Schools, Tulare County, California

"In education, we are always looking for 'ready resources'. This is a practical resource in an easy-to-use format. *Kick-Start Your Class* is the new side-by-side for teachers."
—Shon Joseph, principal, John Tyler High School, Tyler, Texas

"LouAnne Johnson has a unique and effective style in sharing appropriate student-centered strategies. This is a useful guide in every teacher's daily planning for icebreakers and engaging activities."
—José A. Santiago Báez, *Institución Educativa, Nets*, Puerto Rico

Kick-Start Your Class

Academic Icebreakers to Engage Students

written and illustrated by
LouAnne Johnson

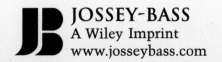

JOSSEY-BASS
A Wiley Imprint
www.josseybass.com

Contents

PART THREE: FORTY WAYS TO WRAP IT UP

*type or
xxxx

x Contents

Acknowledgments

Kate Gagnon is a splendid editor. Her enthusiasm and support for this book truly made it happen. From our first discussion, when *Kick-Start* was just a little idea with big potential, she has included me in every conversation from page layout to cover design and I have never felt more respected or valued as a writer. I "flunked" the only art class I ever took, over forty years ago, and since then I have hesitated to show anybody my "art." Without Kate's encouragement, I doubt that I would have had the confidence to tackle illustrating an entire book—which turned out to be as much fun as it was hard work. I couldn't ask for a better editor than Kate—so I won't.

Also, special thanks to Dimi Berkner and Samantha Rubenstein, who remain ever tactful in the face of my limited (but increasing) technical skills and marketing savvy, and who have taught me how to "blow my own horn" ever so softly, so that I can support their excellent marketing efforts and still remain absolutely charming and incredibly humble.

I could say more about the staff at Jossey-Bass, but in the interest of brevity I will simply say that when other authors ask me, as authors do, if I would recommend J-B as a publisher, I don't have to consider the question. The answer is yes. (*And I'm not just saying that so they will publish my next book. As my Grandma Lauffenberger would say, after a ladylike sniffle, "Don't offer false praise and flattery, Kitten. It makes you look simple, and it's just plain tacky."*)

. . . for all the shy people.

About the Author

LouAnne Johnson is a teacher, author, playwright, and artist who is dedicated to bringing back the joy of learning that children naturally possess before they go to school. While planning the lessons for any class, LouAnne posts her kindergarten photo on the wall above her desk, so she can be reminded every day of what it's like to be on the other side of the desk—where teachers can ruin your life.

"I believe it's important to remember that powerless feeling," she explains, "because it makes me a more compassionate teacher." LouAnne is best known for her work with the at-risk high school students portrayed in her memoir, *My Posse Don't Do Homework* (retitled *Dangerous Minds*, following the 1995 movie adaptation starring Michelle Pfeiffer). But during the past twenty-five years, LouAnne has also taught AP high school students, adult and high school remedial readers, struggling elementary readers, adult ESL students, honors-level freshman composition students, adult developmental readers and writers, university technical writing and literature students, and teacher candidates.

"One of the most important lessons my students have taught me over the years is not to take teaching so personally," says LouAnne. "Teaching is not about me. For example, it may suit me to tell students to find partners, interview them, and introduce them to classmates. But for many students, that activity is a nightmare. They find it very stressful to approach strangers, they get left out of the choosing and feel ostracized, they dread having to speak in front of the class. That's why it's so important for teachers to design student-centered, student-friendly activities that create a welcoming, nonthreatening environment on the first days of class. If we want students to come to school, we must make school a place they want to be, especially that first day. We will have plenty of time later to scare our students, if that's the approach we feel we need to take."

LouAnne devotes an entire chapter ("Start with a Smile") to creating the best possible first day of school in her book *Teaching Outside the Box: How to Grab Your Students By Their Brains*, because she truly believes that the first minutes of class set the tone for the rest of the term. The highlight of the first day is the academic icebreaker—such as those suggested in this new book.

LouAnne's educational degrees include a BS in psychology, an MAT in English, and a doctorate in educational leadership. She is a former U.S. Navy journalist, Marine Corps officer, ballroom dance instructor, and news syndicate editor. She has written several books about education, a number of poems and op-ed columns, and many plays, including the one-person monologue based on her award-winning young adult novel, *Muchacho*.

She maintains a website with a monthly blog and direct links to resources for teachers at *www.louannejohnson.com*. LouAnne also has a website devoted to ideas and resources for the first days of school at *www.KickStartYourClass.com*.

Introduction

FAST, EFFECTIVE, AND FREE

Instructors, coaches, workshop leaders, even preachers use icebreakers—because they work. They put people at ease, create positive brain chemicals, generate enthusiasm, promote interpersonal bonding, create positive emotions, and engage the brain.

Icebreakers are a perfect teaching tool. In just five to fifteen minutes, a properly planned academic icebreaker can:

- → Engage students mentally and emotionally

- → Reduce student anxiety

- → Encourage critical thinking

- → Create a unified classroom community

- → Establish positive teacher-student rapport

- → Bridge economic, social, and cultural boundaries

- → Introduce an academic subject

- → Establish the teacher's authority

- → Promote cooperative behavior

- → Set the emotional "climate" of the classroom

- → Create positive attitudes toward school and learning

. . . and all this while students are having fun!

Time is critical, especially in today's classroom, but icebreakers are worth the time spent because the payback is huge. Any veteran teacher will tell you that the first few minutes of the first day of class are critical—the better those first few minutes, the better the rest of the year. This notion isn't simply anecdotal or logical. It's biological.

The human brain is wired to seek novelty (scientists believe this is a carryover from our ancestors, who had to stay alert for any new danger in order to survive). Regardless of the age or ability of students, their brains all operate in the same way. They seek connections to previously stored information and constantly search for personal meaning. Icebreakers can help younger students create those mental connections between old and new information and experiences. And they help students of all ages create positive personal connections associated with learning.

Emotional memories are stored, just as knowledge and skills are stored, in our long-term memories and can be triggered by current events and experiences. In his book *How the Brain Learns* (Corwin Press, 2001), author David Sousa explains that the amygdala (the emotional control center of the brain) links emotional memory to cognitive memory. When students retrieve academic information, their emotional memories are also retrieved. So it makes sense that creating positive emotional memories associated with school may, over time, supplant previous negative memories and improve students' attitudes and behavior. Of course, it takes more than one positive experience to replace a series of negative ones, but every experience counts.

WHAT CONSTITUTES A GOOD ACADEMIC ICEBREAKER?

First, a good classroom icebreaker has a purpose aside from entertaining students. Simply providing paper and markers and allowing students to doodle, for example, may keep them occupied, but unless you are teaching an art therapy class, that time could be better spent achieving an objective such as learning students' names or creating work teams for future classroom projects and lessons. A good academic icebreaker also meets the following criteria:

→ Can be completed successfully in five to fifteen minutes

→ Involves and engages every student in the class

→ Avoids putting shy students "on the spot"

→ Respects cultural and gender issues

→ Fosters community rather than competition

→ Is ungraded but valued by the teacher

→ Focuses on personalities—not grades or IQs

There is another important factor to consider when choosing first-day activities for the classroom: students are not adults or confident salespeople or corporate conference attendees seeking opportunities to network. The younger they are, the more worried students may be about starting a new school term or meeting new classmates. Good first-day activities do not create more anxiety; they create nonthreatening opportunities for students to share and explore.

ICEBREAKERS CAN INSPIRE LEARNING

Occasionally, students will become so involved in a specific project that you may choose to let them continue for a longer period than you had planned—which follows Maria Montessori's theory that when student learning is taking place, we shouldn't interrupt that learning to suit the teacher's needs. And effective icebreakers can be used as the first step in longer, more complicated projects. Consider the following examples.

High school students can draw self-portraits and post them on a bulletin board to create a classroom community. Later in the week, these same portraits can be used for a variety of purposes: shuffle them and deal them out in pairs or threes to create work groups. Or give all the portraits to a volunteer and see if he or she can correctly identify each classmate by handing the portraits to their proper creators. The portraits can then be used as a springboard for research into the cultures and ancestors of students in the class, an exploration of folk art, or a basis for research into world history with emphasis on the native countries of students' ancestors.

Elementary students can create paper quilt squares during the morning and then take a minute to share and discuss their squares with classmates. Later, they can string or tape their squares together to create a classroom quilt. And in following days, they can draw or use picture cutouts to create a variety of quilts for a variety of topics: colors in the rainbow, numbers, spelling words, pets, wild animals, plants, and so on.

CREATE AN ATTENTION GETTER

One of the best pieces of advice I ever received as a beginning teacher was, "Never yell at students to get their attention or cooperation. It's like trying to teach a pig to sing. It irritates the pig, it makes you look foolish, and it doesn't work." So I tried other techniques. I slapped my ruler against my desk, cleared my throat, circulated the room and used body language to intimidate students into silence. I used those techniques for years and they worked. Sometimes. Then I happened upon a videotape of an elementary teacher from England who used a rainstick to capture his students' attention. Not only did the soothing sound get the students' attention, it made them smile. The following day, I went out and bought a rainstick and I have used it for every class, every age, every ability level, with the same positive results: students like it, I maintain my dignity, and it works.

Rainsticks are South American musical instruments made from a length of cactus that has been dried and coated with shellac. The thorns of the cactus have been turned around so they protrude inside and the hollow stick is partially filled with pebbles that sound like raindrops as they fall when the stick is inverted. This website shows how to make an inexpensive rainstick-style device: *http://www.exploratorium.edu/frogs/rain_stick/index.html*.

What Should You Use?

Your Attention Getter should suit your personality and those of your students. Experiment with noises and musical sounds until you find one that creates an attention-getting sound loud enough to be heard above normal conversation but not loud enough to startle students. Whistles and buzzers work well in a gymnasium, but they can be irritating in a classroom and defeat the purpose of using the sound to request students' calm, quiet attention.

Some good examples of gentle noisemakers include chimes, maracas, a string of tiny bells, five to ten seconds of a song, a tambourine, a wooden frog that "croaks" when a wooden mallet is rubbed across the ridges on its back, a pair of drumsticks, or wooden spoons. Or create your own "music" using objects in your classroom.

Introducing Your Attention Getter

The first time you use your device or signal, let it demonstrate its effectiveness before you say anything about it. Choose a time when students are chatting to each other, such as at the start of class, or when they are working independently and quietly talking to each other. If you are using a signal such as one hand in the air, raise it and wait until students notice. Give them a nonverbal signal that you would like them to raise their hands. When they do, acknowledge them one by one, with a "thank you." If you chose a sound signal, make the sound and wait. Repeat if necessary until everybody is quiet and looking at you. Thank them.

Next, explain that nobody likes wasting their time, and no one really likes it when people raise their voices at us and order us around, even if they state the order as a request such as "Please be quiet." So you will be using a signal or sound to indicate that you need everybody's quiet, calm attention because you have something you want them all to hear. Thank them again for their cooperation and immediately transition to a lesson or activity.

Be sure to use your Attention Getter a few times on the day that you introduce it, so that it becomes a habit for students to stop talking and pay attention. But be sure that when you do request their attention, you have something to tell them. Don't simply ask them to be quiet just to find out if your signal works. Give additional instructions about the current activity, present a new activity, explain a homework assignment or classroom procedure, or let them know how long they have to complete their current task.

Attention-getting sounds and signals are good examples of using behaviorism in a positive way. Students quickly develop the habit of stopping to pay attention when they hear or see the signal. This does not mean you are teaching them to mindlessly obey orders. Rather, it is a mindful exercise. Without speaking, you are saying, "Please listen to me," and students are responding with a nonverbal, "We are listening."

Most teachers continue using the same attention getter with good results, but sometimes teachers (or students) prefer variety. In that case, choose and introduce your new sound or signal just as you did the original one—use it first and then explain. Also, you might consider inviting students to suggest hand or sound signals. If you try one that doesn't work well, don't simply abandon it. Make its failure a topic of class discussion: *Why didn't that signal work? Can we tweak it to make it more effective? What could we use instead?* This discussion will encourage your students to engage in self-reflection about their own behavior and learning—as the result of a mistake! That's good teaching.

HOW THIS BOOK WAS BORN

The most popular assignment in my Effective Teaching courses is the First-Day Activity Demonstration. Using fellow classmates as "students," each future teacher leads us through a quick and easy activity (five to fifteen minutes) designed for a specific grade level and/or subject. In addition to being enjoyable and engaging, the activity has to have some academic purpose such as teaching classroom routines, assessing student attitudes toward an academic subject, or introducing students to each other. This assignment provides valuable practice for new teachers: designing a brief lesson plan, greeting a new class, giving instructions, distributing materials, and practicing classroom management skills such as managing time, monitoring behavior, and motivating students.

As each new group of future teachers works on this assignment, we search for suitable activities online and in textbooks. Although an Internet search yields many sources of free icebreakers, most of them are not really suitable for classroom use. The activities may be enjoyable, but they usually lack any real purpose and often require elaborate materials or more time and money than teachers can spare. Often the instructions are complicated or confusing.

So we turn to the teacher's best resource: other people. We ask our friends and families and students and colleagues to share their experiences as students on the first day of school. And we reflect upon our own experiences as elementary, secondary, and college students. We discuss and analyze the activities we especially enjoyed, as well as those we definitely would not want to repeat. We ask ourselves: *What made those activities enjoyable or terrible? How can we improve them or modify them to suit a different age or ability level?* And then we design our own first-day activities.

Because class after class of my students has such a difficult time finding really good opening activities, I created this collection of first-day activities specifically for teachers. I call them academic icebreakers because every activity included here has a specific purpose and relevance for classroom teachers. They use minimal materials, involve every single student, and are designed to be completed quickly and easily. Every activity included in this collection can be modified to suit a variety of student ages and ability levels. The activity format (consisting of teacher preparation steps followed by specific instructions for students and possible variations) was suggested by my own students—beginning teachers who often struggle to frame clear and effective instructions. "Please give us a script," they said, "so we can just pick a page and do the activity."

Part One of this book presents activities that contribute to an effective classroom: assigning work partners, getting acquainted, learning while moving, and so on. The activities in Part Two are grouped by subject area: math, science, language arts, reading, social studies, technology, arts, music, and English language learners (ELLs). The forty closure activities offered in Part Three—twenty daily and twenty end-of-course activities—are meant to provide templates for teachers who want to wrap up their classes on a positive note and inspire their students to continue thinking about what they have learned.

Many of the activities here were created for my own students. Some are updates of old standards from my school experiences from the 1950s, but most icebreakers are like recipes that pass from person to person by word of mouth, each teacher adding his or her own special ingredients. When somebody mentions an icebreaker, other people usually respond, "Oh, I know that one, except we did it a little differently . . ."

Surely the activities in this book will be improved and revised and passed on, because teachers are eager to share their successful strategies. It's one of the things I love most about teachers—their generosity. After you test these activities and tweak them, edit them, and adapt them for your particular student population, please share them with your colleagues, post them online, and pass them on. Keep that generosity alive.

Kick-Start Your Class

PART ONE

Getting Personal

Creating a Positive State

According to brain scientists, research suggests a phenomenon called "state-dependent learning," meaning that the learning environment plays a key role in the retrieval of previously learned information and skills. Examples of this phenomenon are the way we tend to recall distinct memories from years past whenever we hear a particular song or smell—Elvis singing "Love Me Tender" or the unmistakable aroma of Grandma's homemade cinnamon-pecan buns.

Classroom icebreakers can take advantage of this human tendency to relate memory and emotion by creating positive emotions through enjoyable activities at the start of a new course or school year. In this part of the book, you'll find activities that focus on students as people and members of a learning community. The goal of these activities is to get acquainted with your students and give them an opportunity to learn a bit about you and their classmates via fun and engaging activities that are not physically or emotionally threatening.

Since our goal on day one is to create a welcoming classroom environment and generate positive feelings about our academic subjects so students will look forward to returning for day two, our ideal icebreakers will be specifically designed to reduce potential anxiety or negative stress for students, including newcomers or shy souls.

After your students have had time to bond with you and with each other, they may welcome activities that ask them to stretch their boundaries, tackle tougher challenges, and take more risks. But for the present, the activities in these first five chapters provide the maximum amount of enjoyment and the least amount of emotional risk.

Chapter One, *Getting to Know You: Introductions*, outlines activities that give teachers and students a chance to get acquainted and share a bit about themselves.

Chapter Two, *Working Together: Assigning Pairs & Partners*, provides quick and easy activities for randomly assigning pairs or teams. Random assignment avoids the hurt feelings and conflicts that can occur when students self-select their partners. These activities make a good lead-in to partner projects and tasks.

Chapter Three, *Body & Brain: Kinesthetic Activities*, focuses on activities that incorporate movement. They are a good way to expend excess energy and channel it in a positive direction, as well as serving as good pick-me-ups for the brain.

Chapter Four, *How We Do Things: Routines & Rules*, includes enjoyable ways to present rules and teach procedures.

Chapter Five, *Teamwork: Building Classroom Communities*, includes activities that promote community building and student bonding that can improve behavior, motivation, and achievement.

Working with 'Hard-Core' Students

Sometimes teachers who work with reluctant learners or other challenging student populations are hesitant to use icebreakers. "What if nobody participates?" one teacher asked me. "Then I will look like a fool and I'll totally lose whatever authority I had managed to establish up to that point."

That teacher's question is valid. Some groups of students are much more difficult to motivate and manage than others. But it can be done. The key is to keep in mind the needs of your students. At-risk or underachieving students often have serious self-esteem problems. Their number-one priority is to maintain their "cool" reputations or to avoid becoming vulnerable in front of their peers. They need to feel emotionally safe and protected. So asking them to participate in a round-robin exchange may not be the best choice. You may be surprised at their willingness to participate, however, if you select an activity that is interesting, mentally intriguing, and does not put individual students in the spotlight or ask them to reveal personal information about themselves.

I have used many of the activities in this book with hard-core at-risk students in three different states with good success. The icebreakers that worked best for those groups include I Have to & I Can't, Magic Eyes, Do You See What I See?, and Right or Left Brain? from Chapter One; Puzzle Partners from Chapter Two; My Kind of Class and You & Me Pact from Chapter Four; and Find the Teacher, First-Day Feelings, Paper Turnover, and Unusual Measures from Chapter Five.

Don't underestimate your "tough audiences." It's hard work to maintain an apathetic front and pretend that you don't care about anything in the world. Given the chance to participate without losing face, most students will give it a try. They may still insist that they don't care and that they aren't having fun, but as long as they are participating or not disrupting the activity, they're connecting. (And whatever you do, don't point out that they are cooperating or enjoying themselves! They might decide to stop.)

Don't Forget Your Attention Getter

If you haven't yet read the Introduction, you might want to check out the section titled "Create an Attention Getter." These signals let students know you need everybody's quiet attention or that a specific period of time has passed without having to raise your voice or waste precious time. Attention Getters are especially useful during icebreakers or other activities that students become so engaged in and excited about that they lose track of time.

Chapter One

Getting to Know You: Introductions

We've all been there: the teacher tells us to pair off, interview our partners, then introduce them to the class. And we do it.

Some of us enjoy the activity. But many of us, given the choice, would prefer to be somewhere else, doing something else, something less stressful and more enjoyable—having a root canal at the dentist, for example. Perhaps that's an exaggeration, but only a slight one. Shy people, quiet people, listeners, and introverts often find the prospect of physical pain less threatening than the potential embarrassment and humiliation that may result from speaking in front of a group of strangers or peers. Adults have options. We can escape to the restroom, fake an emergency phone call, or simply get up and leave when we feel too uncomfortable. Typically, students don't have those options. They are stuck. They have to disrupt the class or defy the teacher in order to avoid participating in unappealing activities. So they stay and participate. But being physically present in the classroom with us doesn't mean they are "with us." Mentally, they may be far, far away.

Stress-Free Introductions

The academic icebreakers in this chapter are designed to engage students, make them feel welcome, and allow them to mingle and interact in a nonthreatening, nonstressful environment.

Students feel self-conscious for so many reasons: their height, weight, acne, scars, accents, speech impediments, "'bad" hair, lack of friends, fear of bullies, "uncool" clothes or shoes, body or facial hair, physical discomfort caused by raging adolescent hormones, or past experiences with racial or cultural or religious prejudices.

Many teachers sincerely believe that students need to learn to speak comfortably in public. That may or may not be true, but forcing shy or self-conscious students to stand up and speak during the first moments of a new class is not likely to help them develop confidence or comfort; it's much more likely to make them withdraw even more. It may make them wish fervently that they were any place other than school. Definitely not our goal for the first day of class.

It's very simple to research this topic: simply ask the adults you know to recall their first days of school. Ask how they felt about being required to stand up and speak in front of their peers. Most of them will remember very well—and their memories may help you design effective and enjoyable icebreakers for your own students.

1 THE ADJECTIVE GAME

☆ **PURPOSE:** getting acquainted   ☆ **AGES:** 7–adult

☆ **TIME:** 10–30 minutes

☆ **MATERIALS:** dictionary (optional)

PREPARATION

Create a list of adjectives that might be used to describe students (*happy, energetic, worried, musical, lovable, talkative, quiet, sleepy,* and so on). Post your list on the board or project it on a screen where students can see it.

Place chairs or desks in a circle, semicircle, or some other arrangement where everybody will be able to see each other.

Option for teachers who enjoy using humor: Stand by the door to your room and greet students as they enter. Use various adjectives to describe yourself. For example, "Hello, I'm Mr. Dexter and I am *delighted* to see you." "Welcome to my classroom. I'm Ms. Takada and I'm *thrilled* to see so many interesting people joining our class today." Students may laugh at you, but laughter is a good thing.

INSTRUCTIONS FOR STUDENTS

1 Take a few seconds to think of an adjective that describes you today. You might be excited or hungry, for example. This isn't a test and you aren't stuck with this adjective forever. It's just for the purpose of getting acquainted. I have posted a list of adjectives for those of you who would like help getting started.

2 I'll start by introducing myself and giving an adjective that describes me. Then we'll go around the room. When it's your turn, your mission is to repeat all the names and adjectives of the people who went ahead of you. If you get stuck, we will help.

3 Just for fun, you may choose an alliterative adjective—one that begins with the same letter or sound as your first name—such as Musical Malik or Jumpy George.

4 After we have completed a full circuit, I'll ask for volunteers to see if anybody can remember every name and adjective. *[Skip this step if time is an issue.]*

FOLLOW-UP

On the second day of class, ask for volunteer(s) to try and identify all their classmates by name and/or adjective. Or give students a 5-10-minute "quiz" to see how many names they can remember. This is a challenge if they are seated in different places than they were on the first day. Give volunteers—or the class—a round of applause.

Take note of the people who remember all or most of the names. Those students exhibit strong interpersonal intelligence, a key factor in academic, professional, and personal success, according to many researchers. They may be good team leaders or student mentors.

Taken from *Kick-Start Your Class: Academic Icebreakers to Engage Students.* Copyright © 2012 by LouAnne Johnson. Reproduced by permission of Jossey-Bass, an Imprint of Wiley. www.josseybass.com.

2. AUTOGRAPH COLLECTORS

 PURPOSE: getting acquainted    AGES: 7–adult

 TIME: 10–30 minutes, depending on number and age of students

 MATERIALS: custom templates (see Preparation below) and colored pencils

PREPARATION

Create a template that lists the names of all the students in your class in a column on the left-hand side of the page. Add your name to the list (this will require each student to talk to you individually, which will give you a chance to meet them in a nonthreatening circumstance).

Mix up the order, so the names are not listed alphabetically. Remove any personal information such as ID numbers, phone numbers, birth dates, and so on. To the right of each name, draw two blank lines that students will fill in during the activity.

Greet students as they enter the classroom and hand each student a copy of the template and a pencil. Ask them to be seated and wait for everybody to arrive. Do not tell them your name. They will need to find out when they begin the activity.

Prepare your Attention Getter (see the Introduction for details).

INSTRUCTIONS FOR STUDENTS

1. You have a list of all the names of the students in this class. My name is also included.

2. Your job is to identify each person on the list and ask him or her to sign on the first blank beside his or her names.

3. On the second blank, ask the person to write their favorite after-school snack.

4. You will have __ minutes to locate all the people and collect their autographs and information.

5. The pencils are yours to keep as my welcome gift.

6. This will be the signal that time is up. *[Demonstrate your Attention Getter.]* I'll use this signal whenever I need your quiet attention. Ready? Begin.

(continued)

(continued)

FOLLOW-UP

When you finish the activity, give yourselves a round of applause—this creates very positive brain chemicals. The day following this exercise, ask for student volunteers to try to identify each classmate by name.

You can use the information about snacks to provide favorites during special occasions. (If students list unhealthy snacks, consider offering healthier versions and explaining the strong connection between nutrition and brain function.)

VARIATION

Add more blanks to the template and ask students to share more about themselves—nicknames, hobbies, favorite music or movies, and so on.

AUTOGRAPH COLLECTORS

3. ARE YOU KIDDING?

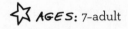

☆ **PURPOSE:** getting acquainted   ☆ **AGES:** 7–adult

☆ **TIME:** 10–30 minutes, depending on number and age of students

☆ **MATERIALS:** template (optional)

PREPARATION

Optional: Create a template with a space for the student's name and two numbered blanks. Distribute the template and give students five minutes to fill it out.

Place your desks or chairs in a formation where everybody will be able to see each other so students don't have to stand up when it's their turn to speak.

INSTRUCTIONS FOR STUDENTS

1 We're going to take turns introducing ourselves, but not in the regular way. When it's your turn, tell us your name and then tell us two things about you—but the secret is that only *one* of the things you tell us should be true. Our job is to guess which thing is true.

2 You could say, "I ate scrambled eggs for breakfast and I like green chile burritos." Or "I have a dog named Hank and I used to live in New York." You can choose how personal you want to be. Keep it clean, of course.

3 After everybody has taken a turn, I will ask you to see how many names you can remember. I'll go first. "I was born in Texas and I drive a Chevy truck."

FOLLOW-UP

When you finish the activity, give yourselves a round of applause—this creates very positive brain chemicals. The day following this exercise, ask for student volunteers to try to identify each classmate by name. Or give students 5–10 minutes to write down as many names as they can remember. This can be a challenge if students are sitting in different locations.

If you use student journals, you can use the activity as a good writing prompt. Ask students to write their response to the activity: *How difficult was it for them to tell when people were "just kidding"? Who did they think had the most interesting things to share? How would they modify the activity, if they have suggestions for making it better?*

VARIATION

This is a variation of the adult game Two Truths and a Lie, where people share two true things and one that isn't true with a goal of fooling the group. If you have older students or more time to spend, you may choose to use that version.

4. BUSINESS CARD CREATIONS

☆ **PURPOSE:** getting acquainted ☆ **AGES:** 6-adult

☆ **TIME:** 10-20 minutes, depending on number and age of students

☆ **MATERIALS:** card stock or index cards, pens or markers, quiet signal, business card templates (optional)

PREPARATION

Cut card stock or index cards to a size appropriate for your students—the younger the student, the bigger the blank "business cards" should be.

Assemble a collection of real business cards to display. Use the Internet to get examples of interesting cards from around the country or around the world.

Before you distribute blank business cards to students, demonstrate your Attention Getter, which will mean time is up or that you need everyone's quiet attention.

INSTRUCTIONS FOR STUDENTS

1 Let's take five minutes to look at the samples of business cards. See how many different kinds of information they display. And while you are looking at the cards, think of things that you like to do or talents you may have. Maybe you are really good at coloring pictures in your coloring books or you can make a great grilled cheese sandwich. Or you know how to design web pages or do tricks on a skateboard. *[Of course, your examples will be adapted to suit your students' ages and abilities. Use your Attention Getter to bring the students back to their desks.]*

2 Now you have 10 minutes to create your own business card. It's your choice whether you want to create a "real" card based on real information—or a "fake" card based on something you think would be fun to do. Be sure to include a picture or description of your business and a phone number or e-mail address so people can contact you.

FOLLOW-UP

When students are finished, ask them to share their cards with the class—or post their cards on the bulletin board and give everybody a few minutes to view them.

VARIATIONS

If your students are older and you have computer access, have them draft a sample card one day. The next day they can create their cards on the computer and print them out on paper or actual business card templates. To build on this activity, you could design a "business conference" where students meet and greet each other and learn how to network (not just collecting names, but filing them under specific topics for future reference—somebody works in film, for example, and somebody else is a technology whiz).

5. FLASH FIGURES

☆ **PURPOSE**: art icebreaker   ☆ **AGES**: 7–adult

☆ **TIME**: 10–20 minutes

☆ **MATERIALS**: flash figure templates on paper or card stock, multicolored markers

PREPARATION

Prepare a template with the outline of a basic human figure. Make copies of the template for students. Make a few extra templates for unexpected arrivals or for students who "mess up" their figures and need to start over.

Create two or three sample finished figures, with faces and clothing added. On one sample, write words to represent favorite hobbies and interests. On another, use only illustrations such as various animals, books, or sports equipment.

Prepare your Attention Getter (see the Introduction for details).

INSTRUCTIONS FOR STUDENTS

1. We're going to introduce ourselves—but instead of words, we're going to use art.
2. Everybody will begin with the same template because we are all humans and we all share many things in common. [Show the sample template.]
3. But when we finish, the templates are going to look very different. [Show samples.]
4. We're all going to add our names, faces, and clothes, along with words or pictures of things we enjoy.
5. We'll have __ minutes to finish our templates. I will give you a 1-minute warning to let you know it's time to finish up. [Demonstrate your Attention Getter.]
6. Don't panic if you don't have time to finish your figure right now. You can always add to it later.

FOLLOW-UP

As students finish, ask them to post their figures on the bulletin board or wall. When the entire class is finished, allow students to browse and discuss their figures. If students seem talkative and comfortable, invite them to present their figures to the class and explain the various words and illustrations they chose to represent themselves.

For classes where students don't already know each other, collect the templates and give them to a volunteer. See how many templates he or she can deliver to their proper creators.

(continued)

(continued)

   Collect the templates, shuffle them, and randomly select one—ask that student to answer a question about the material currently being studied. Or turn the cards face down and have students select one or more to find out who will be their work partners for a specific assignment.

VARIATION

Provide crayons instead of markers for young children. If they can't draw pictures to illustrate their favorite games or toys, let them write any alphabet letters they may know.

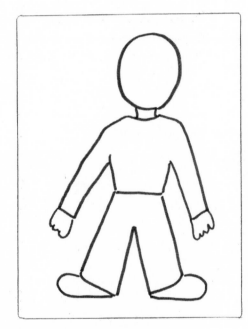

Flash Figure Template

Student Flash Figures

6 GETTING TO KNOW YOU

☆ *PURPOSE*: getting acquainted   ☆ *AGES*: 6-adult

☆ *TIME*: 10-20 minutes, depending on number and age of students

☆ *MATERIALS*: student survey, pens or pencils

PREPARATION

Create a survey that is subject-appropriate and age-appropriate for your students. Include a mix of questions just for fun, questions about study habits and learning preferences, and personal (but not too personal) questions.

    Greet students as they enter your classroom. If you have open seating, hand each student a copy of your survey and a pen or pencil, and ask them to choose a seat. If you have assigned seating, print each name on your roster on a copy of the survey and place the surveys on student desks. As students arrive, greet them and give them pens or pencils. Then ask them to find their own surveys and fill them out. (Have some spare surveys on hand for unexpected arrivals.)

Here are some sample questions:

If you could be invisible for one day, what would you do? (Keep it clean!)

If you could be any animal, what animal would you be, and why?

Would you rather listen to a story, read a story yourself, or never read a story?

How do you prefer to learn a new game?

    a. Have somebody explain how to play.

    b. Watch people play until you get the idea.

    c. Jump right in and learn as you go along.

How do you handle homework?

    a. I do it right away.

    b. I do it at night.

    c. I put it off until the last minute.

    d. I usually forget to do it.

What is your all-time favorite snack?

What can I do as a teacher to help you get a good grade in this class?

(continued)

(continued)

Please circle the activities you like most in school:

    Individual projects

    Discussions

    Group projects

    Doing research

    Writing reports

    Science experiments

    Solving math problems

    Spelling bees

    Group reading

    Individual reading

    Writing journals

    Watching videos

    Portfolios where we work at our own pace

Many teachers find that including an optional bonus question—*What would you like to know about me, your teacher?*—is a student favorite because it gives them a chance to learn something about you. When students view teachers as human beings as well as teachers, it improves communication and encourages mutual respect.

INSTRUCTIONS FOR STUDENTS

1 You will have ___ minutes to complete the surveys. When your time is up, I will give you the quiet signal. *[Demonstrate your Attention Getter—see the Introduction for details.]*

2 If you have any questions, please raise your hand and I will come and help you.

FOLLOW-UP

If time allows, or some time during the next few days, assign students to work independently or in pairs on an interesting, challenging assignment that doesn't require your supervision. Then place a chair beside your desk and invite students, one at a time, to come and have a brief (2-3-minute) private conference with you. If you can't conduct all the interviews on the same day, do a few each day until you have had a personal conversation with each student. Begin each conference by reviewing and discussing the student's Getting to Know You Worksheet. End each conference with a handshake and a smile (even teens who like to pretend they are "too cool" to care about anything may surprise you by being quite personable when they have no audience).

(continued)

GETTING TO KNOW YOU

(continued)

If you added the optional bonus question to your survey (asking students what they might want to know about you, their teacher), select a few student questions to answer at the start or end of each class meeting until you have answered them all. (In the event that students ask inappropriate questions, ignore them. Some students like to show off at the beginning of the term, just to test your sense of humor.)

VARIATION

Ask students to create their own survey and print their name on the back of the survey they create. Collect their surveys and check to make sure there aren't any R-rated questions. Then assign students to work in pairs. You may choose to do an activity from Chapter Two before doing the surveys, so pairs will already be randomly assigned. (If you have an uneven number of students, you or a classroom aide will need to participate.) Have each pair exchange their surveys, and give them 5–10 minutes to complete them and discuss them with each other.

7. I HAVE TO & I CAN'T

☆ **PURPOSE:** getting acquainted   ☆ **AGES:** 6-adult

☆ **TIME:** 10-20 minutes, depending on number and age of students

☆ **MATERIALS:** have to/can't handouts, pens or pencils

PREPARATION

This activity is especially effective for reluctant learners and at-risk groups, because it reminds them that they have the power to choose their own school experience. In a nonthreatening way, it places the responsibility for their learning and behavior on their own shoulders. (If some students choose not to fill in the handout, you can ignore them as long as they aren't disruptive. They will learn just as much by observing as by doing this exercise.)

Create a handout for students that includes the following two incomplete sentences:

I have to _____.

I can't _____.

Place one copy of the handout on each student desk or greet students at the door as they enter the room and give each student a handout and a pen or pencil.

Before you begin the activity, demonstrate your Attention Getter, which means time is up or you need everybody's quiet attention.

INSTRUCTIONS FOR STUDENTS

1. Today we're going to do a short exercise that was designed by a psychologist to help his clients take control of their lives. This exercise is for you. It isn't graded. You don't have to put your name on it or hand it in. And you don't have to share what you have written with anybody.

2. On your handout, you will see two incomplete sentences. Fill in the blanks with the first thing that comes to mind. Don't worry about spelling or grammar.

3. Then go back to your first sentence. Cross off the word "have." Replace it with "choose." Go to your second sentence. Cross off the word "can't" and replace it with "don't want." Now read your two sentences and see if they are true.

4. We often tell ourselves that we *can't* do things, but there are actually very few things in life that we can't accomplish *if* we are willing to do the work. And most of the things we think we *have to* do are really choices—because we don't want to face the consequences of not doing them. There are only five things we truly *have* to do to stay alive: breathe, drink water, eat, sleep, and go to the bathroom. Everything else is optional.

FOLLOW-UP

Ask for volunteers to share their answers. Discuss them as long as you choose. Be prepared for resistance—but let classmates do the arguing. You won't have to.

8. I NEVER WOULD HAVE GUESSED

☆ **PURPOSE**: getting acquainted   ☆ **AGES**: K–adult

☆ **TIME**: 10–20 minutes, depending on number and age of students

☆ **MATERIALS**: none required

PREPARATION

Arrange desks or chairs so that all students will be able to see each other. If you have stationary tables or desks, chairs can be grouped in a large circle.

Prepare your Attention Getter (see the Introduction for details).

INSTRUCTIONS FOR STUDENTS

1 Today we are going to introduce ourselves in an unusual way. In addition to saying our names, each of us is going to share something about ourselves that nobody would guess if they just happened to pass us on the street. This can be something about you as a person or about something you have seen or done: you can wiggle your ears, you once saw a shark, you broke your arm when you were six years old, or you hate chocolate ice cream.

2 Let's take 2 minutes to think of something that nobody would guess about us. Then we'll begin.

3 Okay. I'll go first. My name is _____ and something you probably wouldn't guess about me is: _____.

FOLLOW-UP

Give yourselves a round of applause—this creates positive brain chemicals. Ask for volunteers to see if they can go around and correctly identify everybody by name. Take note of students who can do this—these students have strong interpersonal intelligence. They may turn out to be good leaders or student mentors.

VARIATION

To build on this activity, ask students to write about it in their journals or as short informal essays. Suggested writing prompts: *Which things that other students revealed were the most surprising? The most interesting? How might they modify the activity, if they have suggestions for improving it?*

9. MAGIC EYES

☆ **PURPOSE:** getting acquainted ☆ **AGES:** 6–adult

☆ **TIME:** 10–20 minutes, depending on number and age of students

☆ **MATERIALS:** Magic Eye samples (from a book or the Internet), quiet signal

PREPARATION

Check your local library or bookstore for Magic Eye books that have stereograms with hidden 3-D images that become visible to the naked eye. Or you can print sample pictures from the *www.MagicEye.com* website. If your classroom has computers, you can access a variety of pictures online.

Print and copy the instructions for viewing 3-D images from the *www.vision3d.com* website. They offer three methods, and the majority of students find the second method the most helpful: *www.vision3d.com/method02.html*.

Before you begin the activity, demonstrate your Attention Getter, which will let students know when the time is up or that you need their quiet attention.

INSTRUCTIONS FOR STUDENTS

1 Today we're going to do an experiment using 3-D images.

2 First we'll read some instructions on how to view 3-D images. We'll practice the movements. Then I will give everybody a sample picture. *[Or, if you have computers in the classroom, students can look at images online.]*

3 If you can see the 3-D images easily, please help your neighbors see them.

4 When I give the quiet signal, we will exchange pictures or look at a different image online, because some pictures are easier to see than others.

FOLLOW-UP

Cut several 3-D images from a book or from a calendar and hang them on the wall at student eye level. Students of all ages love looking at the images, and it's actually good exercise for their eyes. When students need a break from sitting or when they finish their work ahead of deadline, let them quietly view the 3-D images.

If you have students who absolutely cannot see the images, you might want to refer them to the school nurse or inform their parents. Research indicates that 10 to 16 percent of children who have convergence insufficiency or double vision are misdiagnosed as ADD (research link: *http://www.childrensvision.com/ADD.htm*). Another good resource on this topic is the College of Optometrists in Vision Development website (*www.covd.org*), where you can read current research or browse links such as Vision & Learning.

10. ME IN A BAG

⭐ **PURPOSE**: getting acquainted ⭐ **AGES**: K–adult

⭐ **TIME**: 5–10 minutes for first session; 10–20 minutes for second session

⭐ **MATERIALS**: small paper bags, markers or crayons, teacher bag

PREPARATION

Please note: this activity takes two sessions to complete.

Collect enough paper bags to offer one bag to each student plus a few spares (lunch bags work well). Write your own name on the outside of your bag and draw a simple design. Inside, place three small objects that have some meaning for you. If you suspect that some students may come from economically disadvantaged homes, include no-cost items—a small pebble, a leaf or flower petal, or a picture from a magazine.

When students are seated, show them your bag. Then show each item and tell them why you placed it in your bag: I brought this photo of my dog because he's my best friend. I brought this leaf because I love trees—I used to climb trees all the time. I cut this picture out of a magazine because it makes me happy to look at it (or because that's the kind of car I want to have some day).

Distribute the paper bags to students. Be sure to give the instructions *before* you distribute the markers, because students (even adults) will stop listening when they have markers in hand!

INSTRUCTIONS FOR STUDENTS

1 After I pass out the markers, I would like you to print your first and last name on the outside of your bag in large letters. Then draw pictures or designs on your bag. Keep it clean. You will have 10 minutes to label and decorate your bag.

2 Tomorrow bring your bag back with three items in it that mean something to you. We will share our bags with the class so we can learn a little about each other.

FOLLOW-UP

On the second day students take turns showing their bags and the items they chose. This can be done as a whole-class activity or in small groups. If some students seem shy, small groups may work best. Shuffle students and repeat two or three times so they have a chance to share with more classmates. After everybody has shared, give yourselves a round of applause.

VARIATION

Instead of paper bags, distribute small cardboard boxes for students to use. The collapsible boxes used for restaurant leftovers are a perfect size.

11. DO YOU SEE WHAT I SEE?

☆ **PURPOSE:** getting acquainted   ☆ **AGES:** 8-adult

☆ **TIME:** 10-20 minutes, depending on number and age of students

☆ **MATERIALS:** sample optical illusion(s), pens and pencils

PREPARATION

Find samples of optical illusions. Label each illusion with a unique title. Make 2-4 copies of each illusion, depending on the number of students you want per group.

Prepare your Attention Getter (see the Introduction for details).

As students enter the room, hand each person a copy of one of the illusions. Ask everyone to be seated and wait for instructions.

INSTRUCTIONS FOR STUDENTS

1. Everybody has a copy of an optical illusion—something that tricks our eyes because it is not exactly what it seems to be. We're going to do a short activity with these illusions to give us a chance to get to know each other.

2. When I give you the signal to begin, you will have __ minutes to locate the other students who have the same optical illusion as yours. Introduce yourselves. Then examine and discuss your illusion.

3. This will be your signal that the time is up. *[Demonstrate your Attention Getter.]*

4. Next brainstorm some possible reasons why your illusion tricks people's eyes.

5. Briefly explain one or two of your reasons, in writing, on the bottom of the page. Please write clearly so others can read your ideas.

FOLLOW-UP

Allow students to circulate around the room, looking at the illusions and explanations. Encourage them to discuss alternative explanations. For more confident groups, ask students to select a representative from their team to share their illusions and explanations with the class.

This activity is a perfect lead-in to a discussion about the importance of thinking—even if you don't get the "right" answer. Sometimes the "craziest" idea leads to the most brilliant answer. If we are afraid to make mistakes, we can miss out on a lot of good learning. Sticky notes, for example, were a mistake involving paper that didn't have enough glue to stick permanently—a million-dollar mistake.

VARIATION

If you have computers and Internet access, students can search online to find sample optical illusions. Then they can print copies or create a digital slide presentation to share their illusion with the class.

12. NAME CARDS

☆ **PURPOSE:** getting acquainted   ☆ **AGES:** K-adult

☆ **TIME:** 10–20 minutes, depending on number and age of students

☆ **MATERIALS:** card stock or heavy construction paper, markers

PREPARATION

Create your own name card by folding a piece of card stock or paper to create a tent shape that will stand up on its own, then printing your name in large letters on it and decorating it with pictures or designs.

Prepare one tent card for each student in your class (and make a few extras for unexpected arrivals).

Count your markers in advance so you know how many to collect at the end of the activity. If you use black Sharpie brand markers, be especially watchful. They tend to disappear—even adults forget to return them—and they may end up being used for graffiti that is difficult to remove from surfaces.

Prepare your Attention Getter (see the Introduction for details).

Place a tent card on each student desk or hand them to students as they enter the classroom.

INSTRUCTIONS FOR STUDENTS

1. First, please print your name in large letters on one side of your tent card. I have already made my card. *[Show them your model card.]*

2. You may decorate your card if you want to—just keep it clean.

3. You will have 5–10 minutes to create your name card. When you hear this signal, it means you have one minute to finish up. *[Demonstrate your Attention Getter.]*

4. After I collect all your cards, we'll test our memories. I will ask for volunteers to see if they can go around and place the correct name cards on the desks of the students who made them.

FOLLOW-UP

Repeat Step 3 on the second, third, and fourth class meetings until students know each others' names. This helps foster a sense of community among classmates. Give a round of applause to anybody who volunteers to try to distribute the cards correctly.

VARIATION

Ask students to list (or illustrate) some of their hobbies or interests on the backs of their name cards. Then collect the cards, draw a random card, and name a hobby or interest. Ask students who share that interest or hobby to raise their hands. Or ask if they can correctly guess whose card you are holding.

13. RIGHT OR LEFT BRAIN?

⭐ **PURPOSE**: getting acquainted   ⭐ **AGES**: 9-adult

⭐ **TIME**: 10-30 minutes, depending on number and age of students

⭐ **MATERIALS**: poster board, brain quiz, Internet access, markers, easel paper

PREPARATION

Brain hemisphere dominance is much more complex than simply saying right brain = creativity and left brain = logic. Both hemispheres analyze data and form thoughts, but they also specialize. The left (analytical) hemisphere handles "hard" facts such as reasoning, science, words, structure, and time. The right (intuitive) hemisphere works with "softer" facts such as color, rhythm, relationships, and humor.

Read Harvard researcher Diane Connell's excellent article for teachers "Left Brain/Right Brain: Pathways to Reach Every Learner" online at *http://www2.scholastic.com/browse/article.jsp?id=3629*. Since teachers tend to lead with methods that suit our own brain dominance, she offers suggestions to expand our teaching repertoires to include methods that will reach more students.

Copy and paste one of the many hemisphere preference quizzes available online (see two resources in the Variations section here) or select questions to create an age-appropriate quiz for your class. Make copies for students.

Create two posters and label them as "List #1" and "List #2." *List #1: Listen to the teacher, discuss things, do research, work by myself, solve problems. List #2: Build things, make models, work in groups, draw my own pictures.*

Next, display the posters on opposite sides of the room.

On separate sheets of easel paper, write "List #1," "Middle," and "List #2" at the top of the page. Provide markers for students to add their names under one of these headings.

Optional: Prepare two short activities: one that requires left-brain skills, such as a logic problem or brain teaser, and one that requires right-brain skills, such as drawing a picture of a scene from a familiar story or making a model to show a process.

Before you begin the activity(ies), demonstrate your Attention Getter to indicate that time is up or that you need everyone's quiet attention.

Do not distribute quizzes until after you have completed Step 3 in the next section. If you provide the handout early, many students will stop listening to you and start reading.

(continued)

(continued)

INSTRUCTIONS FOR STUDENTS

1. There are two posters in the room that list some activities we do in school. When I say "Go," please get up and go read both posters. You'll have 5 minutes. Go. *[After 5 minutes, give your Attention Getter and continue.]*

2. If you prefer the activities on List #1, please go to the easel board with List #1 and print your name. If you prefer the activities on List #2, print your name under List #2. If you enjoy some activities from both List #1 and List #2, print your name on the Middle list. Then please sit down.

3. Now we're going to take a short quiz—not for a grade—but to find out which side of your brain is dominant. Just as most of us are left-handed or right-handed, we also have a dominant brain hemisphere. And just as some people are *ambidextrous*, meaning they can write equally well with both hands, a few people rely equally on both sides of the brain. We also have a dominant ear and a dominant foot. But right now, let's focus on our brains. There are no right or wrong answers on this quiz—just choose the answers that are the most true for you. *[Distribute the quizzes.]*

FOLLOW-UP

Using language and visuals appropriate for the age and ability of your students, discuss brain dominance and how it affects the way we learn. Explain that lessons in your class will include activities that encourage both left- and right-brain thinking.

If time permits, do your left- and right-brain activities. Or save those activities for the next class meeting.

Compare the quiz results with the lists on the easel paper that students signed before taking the quiz. Discuss how closely they match. Assign a group portfolio project that requires reading, writing, discussion, art, and hands-on activities. After they have completed the project, ask students to assess which components of the portfolio were the most and the least difficult for them.

This topic is worth spending some time on for three reasons: it's of high interest to students, it encourages students to reflect on their own thinking and learning, and it gives you information about the best way to communicate a complex idea to each individual student and to design lessons that cater to students' preferred learning styles or challenge development of weaker skills. Experts suggest that we encourage students to develop thinking skills in both hemispheres, rather than always relying on the dominant one.

(continued)

RIGHT OR LEFT BRAIN?

(continued)

VARIATIONS

In a computer lab or library where students have Internet access, let students take an online brain dominance quiz. Here are two options:

About.com offers a short, 20-question quiz that is geared for teens, but younger students may also find it accessible:

http://homeworktips.about.com/library/brainquiz/bl_leftrightbrain_quiz.htm

Test Cafe offers a longer, 54-question quiz: *http://www.testcafe.com/lbrb*

Or search online for more websites; many of them offer quizzes. Be selective, though—some are much more scientific than others.

For younger students, adapt some of the questions or offer a selection of activities and note which students prefer to read or draw or listen to instructions before they begin to work. Also note which students enjoy working independently and which prefer social learning.

RIGHT OR LEFT BRAIN?

25

14. WAVE YOUR FLAG

☆ *PURPOSE*: getting acquainted   ☆ *AGES*: 6-adult

☆ *TIME*: 10-20 minutes, depending on number and age of students

☆ *MATERIALS*: construction paper, markers, scissors, glue sticks or tape

PREPARATION

Assemble a collection of flags from different U.S. states, including the state where your school is located. Tack the flags to the bulletin board or hang them on a cord along a wall or suspended from the ceiling.

Prepare your Attention Getter (see the Introduction for details).

As soon as students are seated, ask if anybody recognizes any of the state flags. Ask if any students have lived in other states. Discuss how each state's flag represents an attitude or philosophy, such as "Don't Tread on Me" or "The 'Show-Me' State." Also discuss animals and plants used as symbols—eagle = freedom, dove = peace, rose or heart = love.

Do not distribute supplies until *after* you have given instructions. People find it hard to listen attentively while they are holding scissors.

INSTRUCTIONS FOR STUDENTS

1 Today we're going to make our own flags. Your flag should represent you in some way: a favorite hobby or interest, or something about your personality. Please print your name on the front or back of your flag to identify it.

2 You will have __ minutes to create your flag. You may ask your neighbors for suggestions or help.

3 When you hear this signal, it means the time is up. *[Demonstrate your Attention Getter.]*

4 Then we will take turns showing our flags and explaining our designs.

5 After we have all presented our flags, we will hang them on the cord (or tack them to the board) so we can all admire them.

Distribute your supplies now. Or let students help themselves.

(continued)

FOLLOW-UP

Invite students to go to the board and write the names of all the states. See if they can collectively remember all 50 names. If they have spelling questions, encourage them to discuss the questions among themselves or refer to a dictionary, instead of asking you for the answer. This will encourage them to become more independent learners and develop their teamwork skills.

VARIATION

If manual dexterity or time constraints are problems, eliminate the scissors and glue and simply provide markers for students to draw their flags with.

Wave Your Flag Samples

15. STAND BY YOUR MUSIC

☆ **PURPOSE:** getting acquainted   ☆ **AGES:** 6–adult

☆ **TIME:** 5–15 minutes, depending on number and age of students

☆ **MATERIALS:** assorted music CDs, posters of singers and bands

PREPARATION

Display CDs or posters in several areas of your classroom, with each station devoted to a particular musical genre (such as country, rap, pop, hip-hop, jazz, classical, flamenco, and oldies) or particular singers or bands (depending on your geographic location and age of students). Place a blank sheet of paper and a pen or pencil at each station.

Create a CD or playlist on the computer that includes selections from each genre or band. Several minutes before students are due to arrive, play your mix at a soft volume.

Greet your students at the door and repeat the instructions several times as they enter the room, so that each incoming group hears them.

INSTRUCTIONS FOR STUDENTS

1 Please walk around and view the musical selections at each station. Feel free to discuss the music with your classmates.

2 After a few minutes, you'll hear this signal. *[Demonstrate your Attention Getter—see the Introduction for details.]*

3 At that time, please go to the station where you believe the music you just heard is located. *[If you teach teens or preteens, they may complain that your taste in music is terrible. In that case, ask them to humor you and choose the least terrible now. Later, they can instruct you in what is currently "cool."]*

4 You will find a blank sheet of paper at each station. When I give the signal to start, the group at your station will have three minutes to write your names and list as many reasons as you can think of to support your opinion that the music at your station is the best.

FOLLOW-UP

After students have completed their lists, ask each group to share the entries on their list or, if your group is a bit rowdy, collect the papers and ask students to be seated. Then you can read out the names from each paper and ask students to raise their hands as you read their names. Ask for volunteers from each group to explain their statements in support of their favorite music. This discussion can take many directions and may provide inspiration for a student debate, private journal writing, or informal essays.

VARIATION

Instead of music stations, create food, animal, or sports stations.

16. WOULD YOU EVER?

☆ **PURPOSE**: getting acquainted   ☆ **AGES**: 6–adult

☆ **TIME**: 10–20 minutes, depending on number and age of students

☆ **MATERIALS**: poster board or heavy paper

PREPARATION

Using poster board or heavy paper, create three individual signs, printed in large letters: "Yes," "No," and "Maybe." Place each sign in a different area of the room, as far apart as possible. Make sure they are big enough to read at a distance.

On the board, write "Would You Ever . . . ?" in large letters.

On index cards, or in a digital slide show, create several thought-provoking questions, such as: *Would you eat a live bug for $100? Would you ever tell a lie to your best friend? Would you ever lie to the police? Would you go to school naked for $100,000?*

Prepare your Attention Getter (see the Introduction for details).

INSTRUCTIONS FOR STUDENTS

1. I am going to ask a series of questions. After I ask each question, you will have 15 seconds to move to the Yes, No, or Maybe station in the room.

2. Next you will have 30 seconds to introduce yourself to the other students at your voting station. Shake each other's hands, if that feels comfortable for you.

3. When you hear this signal, the time is up. *[Demonstrate your Attention Getter.]*

4. After we vote on five questions, you will have the chance to make up your own questions to ask the class.

FOLLOW-UP

Give students 5–10 minutes, working in pairs or small groups, to write more *Would You Ever . . . ?* questions to ask their classmates. Remind them to keep it clean. Ask students to write about this activity in their journals afterwards.

VARIATIONS

If movement isn't possible or appropriate in your classroom, have students do one of the following to vote:

1. Raise their hands when you ask for Yes, No, or Maybe votes.

2. Hold up a green (for yes), red (for no), or yellow (for maybe) card to vote.

3. Provide markers or crayons and let them write "Yes" in green, "No" in red, and "Maybe" in yellow—then they hold up the appropriate card to vote. Tally the vote totals on the board or computer screen.

Chapter Two

Working Together: Assigning Pairs & Partners

Making Sure Nobody Is Left Out

Using an icebreaker to assign work partners is a dual-purpose strategy. In addition to allowing students to interact in an enjoyable activity, the assignment of partners will mean you are prepared for future lessons that require pairs or teams. The activities in this chapter group students randomly, so that popularity and familiarity are not factors. Best of all, nobody is left out, as sometimes happens when students form groups or find partners on their own.

In a recent class on effective teaching, one of the teacher candidates presented a first-day activity that involved choosing partners. Another student, a woman in her early forties with a few years of teaching experience, ended up without a partner.

"I can't believe how upset I feel," she said. "All semester, everybody has been talking about how important it is that we make sure nobody is left out when we assign partners, and I thought you guys were making a big thing out of nothing. Now that it happened to me, I see how awful it feels, even though I knew it was an accident."

If an adult felt that bad, imagine how a child would feel. After all the apologies and explanations and corrections have been made, it's likely that the student will still hear that doubtful little voice saying, *"Nobody wanted me."* And if the teacher rushed in to save the day by offering to be the student's partner, the voice may become even louder: *"Not only did none of my classmates want to work with me, I had to work with the teacher, which made me look like a loser or a brownie or a reject."* Even if the teacher managed to patch up the problem, that's not the kind of memory we want students to take away from our classes. We want them to look forward to our next class with joyful curiosity. (You can avoid this problem by counting students ahead of time and adding yourself or a classroom aide to the partner selection process ahead of time, so that you are "chosen" just as students are.)

Transition to Tasks

The icebreakers in this chapter create an excellent opportunity to transition to a partner or team task as soon as partners are assigned. You can avoid many problems if you give students a task or challenge to complete as soon as they form their groups. For example, give them five to ten minutes to discuss a question or statement and see if their group can agree on an answer—for example, *"Students should be allowed to drop out of school when they are fifteen years old."* Or assign them a fun but useful task, such as *"Design a report card for teachers that students fill out and send to the principal."* The idea is to get them working together as quickly as possible; this makes good use of time and also prevents the "lag time" when personality conflicts can arise out of anxiety or boredom.

Note: When working with "tough" students, avoid assignments that require sharing of personal information that may make them feel vulnerable and defensive. Keep the focus on ideas, concepts, or facts that require thinking and analysis, instead of feelings.

17. CARD SHARKS

☆ **PURPOSE:** assign partners or teammates   ☆ **AGES:** 6–adult

☆ **TIME:** 5–15 minutes

☆ **MATERIALS:** cards with numbers, symbols or pictures; poster board

PREPARATION

Divide the number of students in your class by the number of members (2–4) that you want per team. Then create sets of 2–4 matching cards to make one set for each team. For an uneven class, tweak the card groups so you have one larger or smaller group. (And be prepared to make allowances for absent or new students.)

Place all the cards in one stack and shuffle it.

On poster board, create a master list that shows a sample card from each set of matching cards with blank lines beside or below each sample where student names will be entered.

Design a 10–15-minute assignment or game for students (such as a jigsaw or crossword puzzle, trivia quiz, or quick art project). Post your assignment on the board or screen.

Distribute one card to each student as he or she enters the room.

Prepare your Attention Getter (see the Introduction for details).

INSTRUCTIONS FOR STUDENTS

1. There are __ number of people who have cards that match yours. When I say "Go," you will have ___ seconds (or minutes) to locate the people whose cards match yours.

2. This will be the signal that time is up. *[Demonstrate your Attention Getter.]*

3. As soon as you have matched up your cards, raise your hand and wait for me to come and record your names.

4. After your names have been recorded, sit down with your partners and begin the activity that is posted on the board (or screen).

FOLLOW-UP

Post a copy of your master list where students can easily view it. As new students arrive, add them to existing teams or create new teams.

If you don't have time for an assignment immediately following this activity, then later, when you want students to work in teams, make your assignment and give students 30–60 seconds to find their Card Sharks partners and get to work.

VARIATIONS

Create your own deck of cards with selected words, symbols, or pictures for a specific subject or grade level: symbols (such as stars, balloons, and apples) for nonreaders or English language learners; musical terms (such as *adagio, pianissimo,* and *forte*) for music students; technology terms (such as *wiki, download,* and *web link*) for computer students.

18. ANIMAL PALS

☆ **PURPOSE**: assign partners or teammates   ☆ **AGES**: 5–adult

☆ **TIME**: 5–15 minutes

☆ **MATERIALS**: index cards, pencils, animal drawings or clip art, poster board

PREPARATION

Using drawings, clip art, or stickers, assemble sets of identical animal pictures (three pictures per animal). If the number of students in class is not divisible by three, create one pair of pictures—or participate in the activity yourself.

Next use index cards to create one card for each student in your class (and be prepared for extra students). Attach one animal picture to each card. Draw a blank at the top of the card for the student's name and two blanks below or beside the picture for classmates' names.

Create a master list on poster board or easel paper with a picture of each animal and blanks for three student names beside or below the animal.

If this is your first-day activity, you may choose to hand each student a card as he or she enters the room. Or distribute cards after students are seated. Either way, show them a sample card that is completed with fictional names. Project this completed card on a screen or walk around to enable all students to view the card.

Prepare your Attention Getter (see the Introduction for details).

INSTRUCTIONS FOR STUDENTS

1 Print your own first and last name on the first blank under the picture of the animal on your card. *[Pause while students write their names.]*

2 When I say, "Go," you will have ___ seconds (or minutes) to find the two people whose animal cards match yours. Print your name on their cards. Ask them to print their names on yours.

3 This will be the signal that time is up. *[Demonstrate your Attention Getter.]*

4 After your team has filled the blanks on your cards, bring your cards to the teacher, who will print your names on the master list. *[Or you can let students print their own names.]*

FOLLOW-UP

Post your master list where it is clearly visible by students. Whenever you want students to work in teams, give them 30–60 seconds to locate their partners.

VARIATIONS

To assign pairs or larger teams, decrease or increase the number of animal pictures in each group. For older students, instead of animals, use names or pictures of cities or countries, or terms for specific subjects. (For math, use circles, squares, ovals, cones, and cylinders; for teaching theory, use Dewey, Montessori, Piaget, and Vygotsky).

(continued)

ANIMAL PALS

My Name: _____

My Partners:
1. _____
2. _____
3. _____

My Name: _____

My Partners:
1. _____
2. _____
3. _____

Master List

1. _____
2. _____
3. _____

1. _____
2. _____
3. _____

1. _____
2. _____
3. _____

1. _____
2. _____
3. _____

1. _____
2. _____
3. _____

1. _____
2. _____
3. _____

1. _____
2. _____
3. _____

1. _____
2. _____
3. _____

ANIMAL PALS

19. PERSONALITY MATCHES

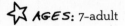 **PURPOSE:** assigning partners   **AGES:** 7–adult

TIME: 5–15 minutes

MATERIALS: card stock or index cards, stickers or line art, poster board

PREPARATION

Using clip art, stickers, or line drawings, assemble pairs of pictures that match a famous person with a title, object, or activity related to that person (athletes and sports, authors and books, singers and songs, actors and movies, and so on).

If you have an uneven number of students, create one trio of matching cards (two books by one author or two movies starring the same actor).

Tape or glue your personalities and titles or pictures to cards.

Create a master list on your poster board with spaces for two names beside or below each personality match you have assembled.

Design a quick activity (word game, math challenge, trivia quiz, or art project) for students. Post this assignment on the board or make instruction sheet handouts.

As students enter the room, hand each student a card or put all the cards inside a bag and invite each student to draw a card.

Before you begin the activity, demonstrate your Attention Getter (see the Introduction for details) to indicate that time is up or that you need everyone's quiet attention.

STUDENT INSTRUCTIONS

1. Your card shows a picture of a person or a picture of an object or activity associated with that person—such as a football player and a football. Your job is to match the correct personality with his or her activity or object.

2. You will have __ number of minutes to find your personality match. As soon as you find your partner, show me your cards so I can make sure you have a proper match. Then you can write your names on the master list.

3. After you record your names, you and your Personality Match can begin your first assignment.

(continued)

(continued)

FOLLOW-UP

Post the master list where students can easily see it. Whenever you want students to work with partners, give them 30-60 seconds to locate their partners and prepare to begin the next activity.

VARIATION

Make this activity more challenging for older students by using abstract or subject-specific matches, such as U.S. presidents and terms of office, or scientists and discoveries or inventions (for example, Newton for gravity, Curie for radioactivity, Jenkins and Armat for the Vitascope).

20. COMICS COWORKERS

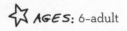

☆ **PURPOSE**: assign partners or team members   ☆ **AGES**: 6–adult

☆ **TIME**: 5–15 minutes

☆ **MATERIALS**: several comic strips, tape dispensers, poster board

PREPARATION

Place tape dispensers in easily accessible locations around the classroom. Arrange desks or chairs in groups of three or four. (Or, if the number of students in your class isn't divisible by three or four, create one or two larger groups.)

Assemble enough unique comic strips so there are enough for each student to have a section after strips are cut into three or four pieces. Write a team name on the back of each strip *before* you cut them into pieces. Cut comic strips into three or four pieces, depending upon how many students you want per team.

On poster board or easel paper, create a master list for names with blank spaces that correspond to the number of teams.

Design a quick 10–15-minute assignment (create a poster, draw their own comic strip, or make a list of everything they know about Australia). Post this assignment on the board or screen, or create assignment sheets.

As students enter your room, hand each one a piece of comic strip and ask them to sit down and quietly wait for instructions.

Before you begin, demonstrate your Attention Getter (see the Introduction for details) to indicate that time is up or that you need everyone's quiet attention.

INSTRUCTIONS FOR STUDENTS

1 When I say, "Go," you will have __ minutes to find the people whose comic strips complete yours. Assemble your comics so they make sense and then tape them together.

2 When you are finished, raise your hand so I can check your names off my roster. Then you can record your names on the master list of Comics Coworkers. Please print your names neatly.

3 Once your names are recorded, you can begin the team assignment.

FOLLOW-UP

Post your master list where students can easily view it. When you want students to work in teams, give them 30–60 seconds to locate their Comics Coworkers and get started.

VARIATIONS

Locate comics with subject-specific content such as history or science. For nonreaders or English language learners, use comics without words or cut them in half to create pairs.

21 PICK-A-STICK PARTNERS

☆ **PURPOSE:** assigning partners   ☆ **AGES:** 6-adult

☆ **TIME:** 5-10 minutes, depending on age and number of students

☆ **MATERIALS:** wood or plastic sticks, paint or markers, poster board

PREPARATION

Divide the number of students in your class by two to determine the number of stick pairs you will need. If you have an uneven number of students, create one set of three sticks. (Be prepared for extra students who aren't on your roster.)

Using markers or paint, create unique pairs of sticks (red polka dots, blue stripes, green dots plus yellow stripes, a white tip and black squiggly lines, and so on).

On your poster board, draw or paint a replica of each stick design and draw two lines below or beside the replica for student names.

Place all the sticks in a box or bag. Create a short, easy task or assignment for students. Post this assignment on the board for older students. Present a demonstration of the task for younger students.

Show students a sample of two matching sticks. Circulate and invite students to draw sticks from the bag or box without looking inside.

INSTRUCTIONS FOR STUDENTS

1 When I say "Go," you will have __ minutes to find the person who has a stick that matches yours exactly.

2 This will be the signal that time is up. *[Demonstrate your Attention Getter—see the Introduction for details.]*

3 After you find your stick partner, bring your sticks to the teacher, who will check your name on the roster.

4 Then print your name on the master list beside your stick design and begin the assignment posted on the board (or handout sheet). *[If students are young, have them sit down after they record their names, so you can demonstrate their partner task or assignment.]*

FOLLOW-UP

Post your master list for future reference. When you want students to work in pairs, give them 30-60 seconds to find their Pick-a-Stick Partners and get to work. Repeat this activity periodically for variety, to mix ability levels, or to prevent personality conflicts.

VARIATION

To use this activity to create teams, create 3-4 matching sticks for each design. If time allows, you can let students paint matching pairs of sticks to use later; this encourages motivation by giving students ownership in the activity.

22. PUZZLE PARTNERS

☆ *PURPOSE*: assigning partners   ☆ *AGES*: K-adult

☆ *TIME*: 5-15 minutes, depending on age and number of students

☆ *MATERIALS*: poster board or heavy card stock, several drawings or photographs, razor or sharp knife

PREPARATION

Glue or paste your drawings or photos to poster board or card stock.

Using a razor or knife, cut each drawing or photo into puzzle form. Cut puzzles into two pieces for pairs or more pieces for teams. Create enough pairs or teams to match the number of students on your roster (and also be prepared for extra students).

On your poster board, create a master list with spaces for student names to be recorded in pairs or teams.

Create a quick task or assignment and post it on the board or create an assignment sheet to hand out.

As students enter the room, hand each one a puzzle piece or invite them to draw a piece from a bag. Before you begin the activity, show a model of a completed puzzle.

INSTRUCTIONS FOR STUDENTS

1. When I say, "Go," you will have __ minutes to find the people whose puzzle pieces match yours. Put your puzzle together and then raise your hand.

2. This signal means time is up. *[Demonstrate your Attention Getter—see the Introduction for details.]*

3. After I check your name on the roster, print your name on the master list along with your partner(s)' name(s).

4. Once you sign the master list, you and your partner(s) can begin working on the assignment. You will have __ minutes to finish. *[For young students, give verbal instructions and a demonstration of the assignment or task.]*

FOLLOW-UP

Post your master list where students can easily see it. When you want students to work in pairs or teams, give them 30-60 seconds to locate their Puzzle Partners.

VARIATION

For young students, cut each puzzle into two large pieces with distinctive colors and designs (a bumblebee or a frog, for example).

Let students create their own puzzles. Before you cut poster board into sections, draw a large X on the back of the board in a distinctive color so you will know which puzzles go together. Cut each blank poster board section into a puzzle with 2, 3, or 4 pieces. Give each student a puzzle piece and colorful markers to decorate it.

23. STORY SEGMENTS

☆ **PURPOSE:** assigning partners or teams   ☆ **AGES:** 7–adult

☆ **TIME:** 5–15 minutes, depending on number and age of students

☆ **MATERIALS:** stories printed on heavy paper, tape dispensers, poster board

PREPARATION

To find the number of different stories you will need, divide the number of students on your roster by the number of students you want to have in each team. To decrease the difficulty of the activity, print out stories with different fonts or on different colors of paper to enable students to quickly identify stories. (For beginning readers, use illustrated stories to provide clues.)

Give each story a unique title. Cut stories into segments, so you have one segment for each student in class. (Be prepared for extra students who aren't on the roster.)

On poster board, create a master list of story titles with spaces for student names to be recorded in pairs or teams.

Place one story segment on each desk or hand each student a segment as he or she enters the room or let students draw them from a bag.

Before you begin the activity, demonstrate your Attention Getter (see the Introduction for details) to signal that you need everyone's quiet attention. Then, if you have younger students, provide a model of an assembled story.

INSTRUCTIONS FOR STUDENTS

1 After I say "Go," you will have __ minutes to find the person (or people) whose story segments match up with yours to tell a complete story.

2 When you locate your story partners, put your story segments in proper order and tape them together. Then raise your hand to let me know you are finished.

3 After I check your story, print your names neatly on the master list beside the title of your story.

FOLLOW-UP

Give students 5–10 minutes to practice, then circulate and have them read their stories to you. Meanwhile, pairs or teams can take turns reading their stories to each other or they can make drawings to illustrate their stories.

Post your master list where students can easily see it. Later, when you want students to work in pairs or teams, give them 30–60 seconds to locate their story partners and get to work.

VARIATIONS

Write your own stories using names of students in your class. Or have students write and illustrate their own stories and cut them into segments.

Chapter Three

Body & Brain: Kinesthetic Activities

Kinesthetic icebreakers are especially helpful for high-energy groups because they channel that energy in a positive direction, but movement is important for any group of students.

As brain research consistently proves, even mild exercise offers big benefits for the brain. Cross-lateral movements—where the arms and/or legs cross over the midpoint of the body—are especially effective in triggering brain function. Cross-laterals are routinely used in physical therapy for stroke and accident victims, but they are equally beneficial for healthy functioning brains.

Neuroscientists such as Eric Jensen, author of *Brain-Based Learning* (Brain Store, 1995), propose that cross-laterals "unstick the brain," activating both hemispheres, because the left side of the brain controls the right side of the body, and the right side of the brain controls the left side of the body. And common sense tells us what scientists and researchers frequently conclude: our brains work best if we take a break every twenty minutes or so.

The icebreakers in this chapter are excellent first-day activities. Some of them (such as *Brain Boosters; Keep It Up; Make Your Move; and Slow, Fast, Slow*) can also be used effectively as "brain breaks" throughout the day.

24. BEANBAG TOPIC TOSS

☆ **PURPOSE:** integrating movement and thinking　　☆ **AGES:** 6–adult

☆ **TIME:** 10–20 minutes, depending on number and age of students

☆ **MATERIALS:** small beanbag(s)

PREPARATION

Clear a space so you and the students can form a large circle (see Variations section for suggestions when working with younger students). As students enter the room, ask them to store their personal belongings and join you to form a circle.

On the board, in large letters, print a topic that is age- and subject-appropriate, such as the solar system, soccer, computers, reptiles, puppies, cars, or math. Or choose a few topics and print them all. Then, during your activity, switch topics from time to time.

INSTRUCTIONS FOR STUDENTS

1 We're going to play a game to give us a chance to get to know each other a little bit. As we play, try to toss the beanbag to somebody who hasn't caught it yet. If you receive the beanbag twice, instead of saying your name the second time, ask "What's my name?" and see how many people can remember it.

2 When you catch the beanbag, you need to do these three things:

→ Say "thank you" to the person who tossed you the bag and repeat his/her name.

→ Say your first name.

→ Tell us something you know about _____ [insert the name of your topic here]. Then toss the beanbag to a classmate.

3 I'll go first. Our topic is math. Let's pretend that Shawna just tossed me the beanbag. "Thank you, Shawna. My name is Miss (Mr.) ____ and I know that a triangle has three sides."

FOLLOW-UP

If students seem to be running out of things to say about your topic, switch to another topic and continue. Switch topics as often as necessary to keep the momentum and student involvement at a high level. Or, when students catch the bag, let them ask a question about the topic that the rest of the class has to try to answer.

VARIATIONS

For very young students, form a few smaller circles with one adult per circle to help facilitate the activity. Complete the activity a few times, shuffling students each time so they have a chance to meet different classmates. Instead of making comments, simply have them say their names and toss the bag to a classmate.

25. BIRTHDAY CIRCLE

☆ **PURPOSE**: integrating movement and thinking   ☆ **AGES**: 6–adult

☆ **TIME**: 10–15 minutes, depending on number and age of students

☆ **MATERIALS**: index cards (optional—see the Variations section)

PREPARATION

Create an area in your classroom with enough room for all the students to form one large circle.

As students enter the room, ask them to store their personal belongings and then stand up. Show them the starting point for your birthday circle.

Before you begin the activity, demonstrate your Attention Getter that means time is up or that you need everyone's quiet attention (see the Introduction for details).

INSTRUCTIONS FOR STUDENTS

1 Your mission is to see how quickly you can form a circle (or line up) with everybody in chronological order by their birthdays, beginning with January 1.

2 If your birthday is in January, please take your place at the starting point. Then talk among yourselves to put yourselves in order by date.

3 After we have formed our circle, we'll go around and introduce ourselves. When it's your turn, please say your name and then tell us something that you think would make a wonderful birthday gift.

FOLLOW-UP

After students have lined up, congratulate them for how quickly they formed their circle—and for cooperating so nicely with each other. Then model the procedure for introductions: "My name is Miss (Mr.) _____ and I would love to get a new puppy for my birthday." Then ask the first student in your birthday circle to introduce himself or herself.

VARIATIONS

If students are too young to know their birthdays, help each student print the first letter of his or her first name on an index card. Then ask them to line up in alphabetical order, with all the As first.

To challenge older students, ask them to print their first names on index cards and then line up in reverse chronological order (December 31 would come first) or reverse alphabetical order, using their entire first names (Zelda would come before Tomas, and Michael would come before Malik).

26. BRAIN BOOSTERS

☆ *PURPOSE*: integrating movement and thinking   ☆ *AGES*: K–adult

☆ *TIME*: 5–15 minutes, depending on number and age of students

☆ *MATERIALS*: none required

PREPARATION

Choose a simple exercise that involves cross-lateral movement—moving your hands and/or feet across the midpoint of the body. These movements are similar to those used by physical therapists who work with stroke victims; they are grounded in brain science and research. You can find sample cross-lateral exercises and scientific rationale for using them online or in books such as Eric Jensen's *Brain-Compatible Strategies* (Hawker Brownlow, 2007). A good starting place for an online search is Dr. Jean Feldman's website: *www.drjean.org/html/monthly_act/act_2006/03_Mar/pg04.html*.

Clear a space for students to do the exercises, or let them stand beside their desks. The sample exercise here is simple: lift your left knee and tap it with your right hand. Then lift your right knee, tap it with your left hand. Practice doing the exercise a few times so you can lead students to do it with you. Six repetitions is a good number to use.

INSTRUCTIONS FOR STUDENTS

1 We are going to do some exercises designed to wake up our brains and help us do our best thinking. First, I will demonstrate the exercise with my back to you so you can follow along with me if you want to. Or you can just watch.

2 Now let's do the exercise together. Lift your left knee and tap it with your right hand. Then lift your right knee and tap it with your left hand. And we'll repeat this combination six times. Ready? Right hand, left knee. Left hand, right knee. Right hand, left knee. Left hand, right knee . . .

FOLLOW-UP

Begin each class meeting with 2–5 minutes of cross-lateral exercises. Ask for student volunteers to lead the exercises. This is time well spent: it lets students burn off excess energy, increases oxygen to their brains, improves hand-eye coordination, and encourages activation of both left- and right-brain hemispheres.

VARIATIONS

Create a combination of 2 or 3 exercises to do once each hour of class time. Change exercises weekly for variety. Exercise outdoors if time and weather permit.

BRAIN BOOSTERS

27. FIND YOUR FOLDER

☆ **PURPOSE:** integrating movement and thinking   ☆ **AGES:** 6–adult

☆ **TIME:** 10–15 minutes, depending on number and age of students

☆ **MATERIALS:** manila or multicolored file folders, markers

PREPARATION

Write the name of each student in your class on the tab of a folder. Keep a few spares. Place the folders on student desks. (Make a sketch for your own reference, if you want to have assigned seating.) Place markers in easily accessible locations.

Optional: Place a handout for students inside the folders—not just a list of rules, but something informative or fun (such as a course outline, a quick assignment, or a brain teaser).

Greet students as they enter. Invite them to locate their seats by finding the folders with their names on them. (If you have unexpected arrivals, quickly create their folders and place them after students have begun the search.)

When everybody is seated, demonstrate your Attention Getter to indicate that time is up or that you need everybody's quiet attention.

INSTRUCTIONS FOR STUDENTS

1 At the start of every class, I will distribute your folders. And I'll collect them at the end. When I have assignments or tests to return to you, I will place them in your folder. If you take notes during class, you can store them in your folder and use them to review for tests.

2 We're going to take __ minutes to personalize our folders—just keep it clean. You'll find markers located around the room. Please share them and use them *only* to write on the folders.

3 *Optional:* Inside your folder, you will find a handout. If you finish decorating your folder ahead of time, you may begin working on the handout.

FOLLOW-UP

Collect the folders and see if you can deliver them all to the correct people. Repeat this until you learn all their names. *Optional:* Ask a student volunteer to try.

VARIATION

As students enter the room, hand them a random folder. When they say, "That's not my name," smile and say, "What was I thinking? Please sit down and hold onto that folder for a moment." After everybody is seated, give them 5–10 minutes to deliver their folders to the proper people. After all the folders have been delivered, collect them, mix them up, and repeat the activity. Repeat until they know each other's names.

28. KEEP IT UP

☆ **PURPOSE:** integrating movement and thinking ☆ **AGES:** 6–adult

☆ **TIME:** 10–15 minutes, depending on number and age of students

☆ **MATERIALS:** balloons

PREPARATION

Create an area in your room—or outside—where there will be enough room for students to move around.

If your students are young, you will want to inflate the balloons ahead of time. Otherwise, they can inflate their own.

As students enter the room, ask them to find a seat and store their personal belongings. Divide students into pairs or teams. *(If students seem hesitant to mingle, you may want to use one of the activities for getting acquainted from Chapter One before using this activity. And you will find quick and easy activities for assigning partners or teams in Chapter Two.)*

Before you begin the activity, demonstrate your Attention Getter that means time is up or that you need everyone's quiet attention (see the Introduction for details).

INSTRUCTIONS FOR STUDENTS

1 When I say, "Go," your mission is to see how long you can keep your balloon afloat— without using your hands. You may use the rest of your body, but be careful that you don't kick or hit another student by accident.

2 You will have one minute to practice, and then we'll start the timer to see who can keep their balloon afloat the longest without letting it touch the ground.

3 Ready, set, go. *[Use your Attention Getter at the end of one minute to get their attention and begin the activity.]*

(continued)

FOLLOW-UP

Ask the winning team(s) to demonstrate their techniques for keeping the balloon afloat. If students are very engaged, repeat the activity or do it again later on.

Take note of which students seem to have especially good hand-eye coordination; they may be kinesthetic learners who respond well to lessons that incorporate movement. Some of them may require movement in order to learn effectively.

VARIATION

Instead of making this a competition, just let students try to keep the balloons afloat without worrying about time. Give them 2 minutes for the activity, then switch partners or teams. Repeat several times so they get to work with different students.

KEEP IT UP

29. HELLO, STRANGER!

☆ **PURPOSE**: integrating movement and thinking ☆ **AGES**: 6–adult

☆ **TIME**: 10-20 minutes, depending on number and age of students

☆ **MATERIALS**: none required

PREPARATION

Translate "hello" or "good day" into several languages *(for example*, ciao *in Italian*, bonjour *in French*, hola *in Spanish*, mabuhay *in Tagalog and*, guten tag *in German)*. Choose languages to represent your students' ethnicities—or increase the challenge by choosing unfamiliar languages.

Create an area with enough space for all the students in class to form two circles, with one circle inside the other.

As students enter the room, assign them a number, alternating number 1 and number 2. If you have an uneven number of students, join one of the circles yourself.

Ask students to store their personal belongings, then form two circles, with number 1s on the outside facing in and number 2s on the inside facing out, so that students are facing each other.

INSTRUCTIONS FOR STUDENTS

1. When I say "Go," your job is to greet the person across from you by saying hello and giving your name—the people in the outside circle will speak first. But since I can tell that you're extremely smart students, we're going to add a little challenge. We're going to say hello in different languages.

2. Before we begin each round, I will give you the word to use—but I won't tell you the country. I will say "hello" and see if anybody can identify the language.

3. Ready? Here's the first hello: *Aloha!* What language is that? *[Hawaiian.]*

4. After you have both said your names, the people in the inside circle will move to their left, so they are facing the next person in the outside circle, say *Aloha*, and introduce yourselves. Then move along to the next person. The people in the outside circle will stay where they are.

FOLLOW-UP

After students complete one cycle, give them one minute to scramble themselves and reform two circles. Then repeat the activity with a different language. Use this activity as a springboard for research projects about culture, language, and customs.

VARIATION

Instead of forming circles, assign students to groups. Give each group a different word for hello. After they shake hands, say hello, and call each other by name, give them a new word. Then circulate and give each group the next word to practice.

30. MAKE YOUR MOVE

☆ **PURPOSE**: integrating movement and thinking ☆ **AGES**: 6–adult

☆ **TIME**: 5–15 minutes, depending on number and age of students

☆ **MATERIALS**: none required

PREPARATION

Clear a space big enough for students to form a large circle and move around without bumping each other.

INSTRUCTIONS FOR STUDENTS

1. We're going to learn each other's names, but to make it more fun we're going to make up our own movements, too. *[If students are young, show the moves as you name them.]* You could stick out your tongue, wrinkle your nose, stomp your foot, clap your hands, wave your arm, jiggle your foot, snap your fingers, shake your head—whatever you want to do. But your move needs to be special, not like anybody else's.

2. When it's your turn, say your name and make your move.

3. I'll go first to show you how it's done. My name is ___ and here's my move. *[Make your move.]*

4. And to add an extra challenge, because I can see that you are extra smart, *before* you say your name, you need to say the names of everybody who went before you and show us their moves. If you forget, we'll help you.

5. Whoever goes first will need to say my name and show my move, then tell us his or her name and show us their move. Ready?

FOLLOW-UP

Repeat this activity periodically. This is time well spent: it lets students burn off excess energy, increases oxygen to their brains, improves hand-eye coordination, and encourages activation of both left and right brain hemispheres.

Note: very young children may not be able to remember other people's movements. That's fine. Just let them say their names and do their own moves.

VARIATION

Do this activity outdoors occasionally, if time and weather permit.

31. MEET AND GREET

☆ **PURPOSE**: integrating movement and thinking   ☆ **AGES**: 6–adult

☆ **TIME**: 10–20 minutes, depending on number and age of students

☆ **MATERIALS**: none required

PREPARATION

Create an area where there is enough space for all the students in class to form two circles, with one circle inside the other.

As students enter the room, assign them a number, alternating number 1 and number 2. If you have an uneven number of students, then join one of the circles yourself.

Ask students to store their personal belongings, then form two circles, with the number 1s on the outside facing in and number 2s on the inside facing out. Students should end up facing each other.

Before you begin the activity, demonstrate your Attention Getter to signal that time is up or that you need everyone's quiet attention (see the Introduction for details).

INSTRUCTIONS FOR STUDENTS

1 When I say "Go," your job is to give the person across from you a high five with your left hand and say, "Hi, my name is ___."

2 After you have both said your names, the people in the inside circle will move to their left, so they are facing the next person in the outside circle, give the high five, and introduce yourselves. The people in the outside circle will stay where they are.

FOLLOW-UP

After students complete one cycle, give them one minute to scramble themselves and re-form two circles. Then repeat the activity, but this time instead of high fives, they do pinkie finger handshakes and introductions. To add a challenge, have students clap their hands twice, then slap hands with the person facing them before they say their names, or clap their hands twice and spin around in place before slapping hands with the other person. Students may suggest other variations.

VARIATIONS

This activity can be done in a variety of ways, with students forming two lines that face each other, or with students in a single line where the first person leads off and greets the second person in line, and the third, and so on, as the other students follow along, greeting each new classmate.

32. NAME GAME BALL TOSS

☆ **PURPOSE**: integrating movement and thinking   ☆ **AGES**: 6–adult

☆ **TIME**: 10–20 minutes, depending on number and age of students

☆ **MATERIALS**: small, soft ball(s)

PREPARATION

Clear a space big enough for you and the students to form one large circle (see Variations section for multiple circles).

   As students enter the room, ask them to store their personal belongings, then join you to form a circle.

INSTRUCTIONS FOR STUDENTS

1. We're going to use a ball toss game to learn everybody's names.

2. When you catch the ball, thank the person who tossed you the ball and repeat that person's name. "Thank you, Jerome." Then say your own name, and toss the ball to a classmate. Try to toss the ball to somebody who hasn't caught it yet.

3. If you do catch the ball more than once, only say your name the first time. On your second or third catch, thank the thrower by name and then ask, "What's my name?" so we can see who remembers.

4. I'll go first. Let's pretend that Hans just tossed me the ball. "Thank you, Hans. My name is ___ ." *[Toss the ball to the first student to begin.]*

FOLLOW-UP

After everybody has had a turn, repeat the activity, but this time students don't say their own names. They thank the person by name who tossed them the ball. Then they toss the ball again and the receiver has to thank them by name. If a student can't remember the tosser's name, they can ask for help from the class.

VARIATIONS

For very young students, form a few smaller circles with one adult per circle to help facilitate the activity. Complete the activity a few times, shuffling students each time so they have a chance to meet different students. Instead of saying thank you, they can just catch the ball and say their own names before passing it on.

Add a challenge for older students by having them make up a fun name for themselves that includes their real first name or nickname. Mike the Mouse Catcher, Super-Duper Shirell, 200-mph Richard, Alvin Little Foot. Write some sample fun names on the board if they need inspiration. They will catch on quickly.

33. NAME TAG SEARCH

☆ **PURPOSE:** integrating movement and thinking   ☆ **AGES:** 6–adult

☆ **TIME:** 10–15 minutes, depending on number and age of students

☆ **MATERIALS:** name tag for each student

PREPARATION

Create a name tag for each student listed on your roster. Be creative. Add stickers or designs to the tags. Make a few spares so you can add the names of unexpected arrivals who are not on the roster. If you do have unexpected arrivals, quickly fill in their names on tags and hide them after students begin their search, so they won't see you.

Hide the name tags around your classroom. (Make a note or sketch for your own reference, to remind you where you hid the tags.) For younger children, make the hiding places more obvious than you would for older students.

After students are seated, demonstrate your Attention Getter to indicate that time is up or that you need everybody's quiet attention (see the Introduction for details).

INSTRUCTIONS FOR STUDENTS

1 I have created a name tag for everybody here. But I must have been absentminded this morning, because I can't seem to find them. I'm sure they are someplace in this room.

2 When I say, "Go," you will have __ minutes to find your name tag. If you find somebody else's tag, your job is to locate that person and give him or her the tag. Then ask that person to help you search for yours.

3. After you have located your tag, help your classmates find theirs.

FOLLOW-UP

Tape the name tags to the legs of their chairs, under their desks, or elsewhere on student seating. This works well for younger students or for those who don't speak English—you can mime the instructions to show them where to look for their tags.

Collect the name tags and ask for a volunteer to see if he or she can deliver them all to the correct people. Give the volunteer a round of applause.

VARIATION

As students enter the room, hand them a random name tag. When they say, "That's not my name," smile and say, "What was I thinking? Please hold onto that tag for a moment." Then, after everybody is seated, give them 5–10 minutes to locate the person whose tag they are holding. After all the tags have been delivered, collect them, mix them up, and do the exercise again. Repeat a few times until they learn each other's names.

34. SHALL WE DANCE?

☆ **PURPOSE:** integrating movement and thinking   ☆ **AGES:** K-adult

☆ **TIME:** 10–20 minutes, depending on number and age of students

☆ **MATERIALS:** music; DVD, VHS, or Internet dance instruction (optional)

PREPARATION

Find a song with an easy cha-cha beat. Learn to do a simple cha-cha step to the left and right. (See online demo.) Practice counting out loud so you can teach students.

Clear a space for students to move without bumping one another. If your classroom is too small, use a corner of the gym or an empty hallway. Or go outdoors.

As students enter the room, invite them to store their belongings and form two or three lines, facing you. (*Straggly lines are fine. Don't be a drill sergeant!*)

INSTRUCTIONS FOR STUDENTS

1. Today, we're going to do the Hello Cha-Cha. I will demonstrate the step with my back to you, so you can follow along if you want. Or you can just watch. *[Demonstrate the step without music, counting out loud: (to the left) one, two, cha cha cha, (to the right) three four, cha cha cha. Starting with your right foot, step in front of your left foot, step back to where you started, then alternate left, right, left. Then, starting with your left foot, step in front of your right foot, step back to where you started, then alternate right, left, right.]*

2. Now we're all going to do the whole sequence four times. Ready? One, two, cha cha cha. Three, four, cha cha cha . . . *[Do one sequence without music, then add music.]*

3. Great! Now, when I say "Go," you will have 10 seconds to say hello to the people on your left and right and tell them your name. Then, we'll do a 5-second scramble so you are standing next to different people and get ready to do the steps again. Ready? Go! *[Wait 10 seconds.]* Five-second scramble! Go!

FOLLOW-UP

Begin each class meeting with 2–5 minutes of dance. Ask for student volunteers to lead the group. Dancing burns excess energy, increases oxygen to the brain, improves hand-eye coordination, and encourages activation of both brain hemispheres.

VARIATIONS

Find instructions online, or on DVD or VHS video, for a simple oldies or country line dance. Show the video and teach your students the step.

Special note: If dance won't work for your culture or community, consider teaching deep breathing yoga exercises designed to calm the mind and center the focus.

35. SYMBOL SEARCH

☆ *PURPOSE:* integrating movement and thinking ☆ *AGES:* 6-adult

☆ *TIME:* 5-15 minutes, depending on number and age of students

☆ *MATERIALS:* name symbol card for each student

PREPARATION

This activity works especially well for non-English speakers and nonreaders.

Use squiggles, dots, circles, squares, flowers, and other designs to create a card that bears a unique symbol for each student on your roster. For younger students, use large designs and bright colors to help them distinguish their symbols. Make a few spares for unexpected arrivals. Make a copy of each card so you have matching pairs.

Tape the original cards to the backs of student chairs or on top of their desks. Keep the copies of the cards in a stack to distribute to students as they enter your room.

Greet students at the door and hand each one a symbol card. Invite them to find their seats by matching their symbol card to the cards on the desks or chairs. If students don't speak English, mime the instructions for them by taking a sample card and searching for its match on one of the seats.

STUDENT INSTRUCTIONS

There are no instructions required if you meet students at the door and direct them as outlined above. Otherwise, provide verbal instructions and a time limit.

FOLLOW-UP

After students are seated, demonstrate your Attention Getter to indicate that time is up or that you need everybody's quiet attention (see the Introduction for details). (If you want to use assigned seats, make a quick seating chart after students have located their seats.)

Begin your introductory lesson or start a new activity.

VARIATIONS

To increase the challenge, tape the symbol cards underneath student desks or seats. Or place them inside copies of the text. Students have to find their matching cards in order to locate their textbooks.

If you want students to work in pairs, create four matching symbol cards for each design. Distribute two matching cards to two different students as they enter (if you have an odd number of students, create one card trio).

(continued)

(continued)

Symbol Search Samples

36. SLOW, FAST, SLOW

⭐ **PURPOSE**: integrating movement and thinking   ⭐ **AGES**: 6–adult

⭐ **TIME**: 10–20 minutes, depending on number and age of students

⭐ **MATERIALS**: none required; music with adjustable tempo is optional

PREPARATION

Design a short sequence of movements such as tapping the knees or elbows, stepping in place, clapping hands, raising arms. Qigong or tai chi movements work very well.

Here is just one of many possible sequences: *bend both knees slightly as you tap your knees with your hands, straighten legs and clap once, raise right hand, clap once, raise left hand, clap once, push both arms out to the sides, clap once.*

Practice your movements until you can do them smoothly and quickly. If you have the ability to play music where you can adjust the tempo, add music to the mix.

Clear an area of the classroom, find an empty hallway, use a corner of the gym or cafeteria, or go outdoors. Or, if your movements don't require a lot of space, simply ask students to stand up and step away from their desks.

INSTRUCTIONS FOR STUDENTS

1 We're going to wake up our brains with an activity called Slow, Fast, Slow. We'll do a series of movements at normal speed. Then we'll slow down to ultraslow motion. Next, we'll go faster until we hit warp speed. Then we'll slow back down to normal.

2 First, I'll demonstrate the movements. You can follow along with me or you can just watch—whichever works better for you. Don't worry about making a mistake. Just let your body enjoy moving. *[Demonstrate your sequence of moves.]*

3 Now we're going to start with three repetitions at a normal speed, so you can learn the sequence. Then we'll slow down until we're in ultraslow motion. *[Begin.]*

FOLLOW-UP

Slow down for each repetition until you reach ultraslow motion. Then increase the speed for each repetition until you reach warp speed. Let students enjoy themselves when they try to move as fast as possible. Then bring the group back together as you slow back down to normal speed.

VARIATIONS

Do this activity daily, using a different sequence for each day (or week). Invite students to create the sequence of movements. To increase the challenge, add a hop or turn to the movements.

SLOW, FAST, SLOW

58

37. VERB MANIA

☆ **PURPOSE:** getting acquainted   ☆ **AGES:** 6–adult

☆ **TIME:** 10–20 minutes, depending on number and age of students

☆ **MATERIALS:** none required

PREPARATION

Create a space in your classroom big enough for everyone to form a circle or two lines facing each other. On the board or projector, provide a list of action verbs such as *wiggle, clap, wave, stomp, jump, shiver, hop, snore, gasp, exhale, stretch,* and so on.

    As students enter your classroom, ask them to store their personal belongings and take their positions in the line or circle. Before you begin the activity, show your students the verb list and ask them if they can give you more examples. When you are certain that everybody knows what a verb is, begin the activity.

INSTRUCTIONS FOR STUDENTS

1 We're going to take turns introducing ourselves and demonstrating an action verb. I'll go first. My name is _____ and my verb is "Whisper." *[Whisper when you say the word whisper.]*

2 When it's your turn, say your name, tell us your action verb, and act it out. But *before* you introduce yourself, you need to say the name of each classmate who went before you and act out their verbs, too.

3 If you forget somebody's name or verb, we will help you.

FOLLOW-UP

Later in the day or on the following day, see how many students can remember all the names and verbs of their classmates. This activity can be repeated frequently if students need to expend pent-up energy. Instead of verbs, you can ask them to demonstrate silent gestures or emotions such as fear, anger, happiness, hope, love, surprise, or worry.

VARIATION

Instead of asking students to name their verbs, ask them to act out their verbs while the rest of the class tries to guess the verb they are demonstrating.

Chapter Four

How We Do Things: Routines & Rules

*E*very teacher has his or her own teaching methods, curriculum requirements, student personalities and classroom logistics to consider, but every teacher shares some common needs.

We all need to find ways to quiet our classrooms, communicate our expectations for student behavior, distribute and collect materials, clean up after projects, check for understanding, respond to unexpected interruptions, and so on. Standard routines and rules can save time and frustration for both teachers and students, and result in a more efficient, more enjoyable classroom environment.

Routines Reduce Behavior Problems

One of the most effective classroom management tools is referred to by various titles such as Do This Now or Bell Ringers. Master teacher Fred Jones, author of *Tools for Teachers* (Fredric H. Jones & Associates, 2000), uses the term Bell Work. The idea is that you provide a specific task or assignment for students to begin each day as soon as they enter your classroom. This encourages a smoother and quicker transition from the social life outside the classroom to the academic focus inside. Students very quickly get into the habit of entering the classroom and settling down to work. For more information on this topic, see Chapter Five in *Teaching Outside the Box* (Jossey-Bass, 2011) or read an article by Fred Jones at *www.fredjones.com /Tools-for-Teaching/bellwork.html*.

Teach your standard procedures one or two at a time and practice them frequently until students can perform them without any guidance or instruction. This not only saves time, but it also helps students develop a sense of responsibility and positive self-discipline.

38. CLASS CHANT

⭐ **PURPOSE:** establishing classroom rules and routines ⭐ **AGES:** 6-16

⭐ **TIME:** 5-10 minutes, depending on number and age of students

⭐ **MATERIALS:** poster board, index cards and pencils (optional)

PREPARATION

Chants can be great motivators. If you think teenagers won't like them, think again. Think about how much people enjoy rituals: repeating favorite phrases, singing the national anthem at ball games, reciting honor codes, Boy Scout and Girl Scout Pledges, sorority and fraternity songs, or the Pledge of Allegiance.

The key to success is to choose a chant that suits the age and personalities of your students. First graders might enjoy: *"Who's the coolest class in school? We are! Who always does their best? We do!"* Ninth graders might prefer: *"Integrity and respect: do the right thing even when nobody is looking."* Or, *"Respect yourself first; the rest will follow."*

In this YouTube clip, first-year teacher Andrea Schindler leads her third graders in a chant, and it's obvious that the students take what they are saying (*"Do your best"*) to heart: *www.youtube.com/watch?v=Z8WpiueGP5s.*

Create a chant for your class. You can find many samples online. Here's a good place to start: *www.songsforteaching.com/chantsraps.htm.*

Print copies or have students write the chant on index cards. Project the words on a screen or print them on the board. Create a poster for the classroom—ask your students to autograph the poster. If you have multiple classes, create multiple chants or posters.

INSTRUCTIONS FOR STUDENTS

1 I have created a special chant just for our class. We'll repeat it every day, and before long we'll know it by heart.

2 Later on, after we know each other better, you will have the chance to create your own chant. But for right now, we'll use the one I wrote for you.

3 Please listen while I read it once. Then we'll all read it together.

FOLLOW-UP

Practice your chant a few times. If students seem especially engaged, see if they want to try to memorize it. Practice it at least once during each class meeting. Add hand motions for younger students. They love the movement.

VARIATIONS

Begin with a class discussion about rituals before teaching the chant. Create a class song instead of a cheer. Ask students to work in pairs or small groups to create their own chants or songs; put all the student suggestions into a hat and select one to use for a month.

CLASS CHANT

39. CALL-AND-RESPONSE

☆ **PURPOSE:** establishing classroom rules and routines   ☆ **AGES:** K-18

☆ **TIME:** 5-10 minutes, depending on number and age of students

☆ **MATERIALS:** none required

PREPARATION

Write a call-and-response script for your class. This idea is based on a musical form where one musician leads with a melody and other musicians respond. It has been adapted as an effective motivational tool by people from preachers to coaches to political activists. Classroom call-and-response has two primary uses: as an attention getter to quiet students or as a motivational technique to generate enthusiasm about learning.

Write your script(s) on the board, project it (or them) on a screen, or create a handout. In the two examples below, T stands for the teacher, and S stands for students:

T: One, two	S: Eyes on you
T: Three, four	S: Talk no more

T: Ears?	S: Listenin'
T: Eyes?	S: Lookin'
T: Heart?	S: Feelin'
T: Brains?	S: Cookin'

The Ears-Listenin' script works well with motions to match the words.
You can find many more examples online. Here are a few to get you started:
www.proteacher.org/c/517_Attention_Signals_-_Call_and_Response.html and
www.futureofeducation.com/profiles/blogs/teaching-techniquecall-and-1

INSTRUCTIONS FOR STUDENTS

1. We have all heard a call-and-response. Here's an example: The coach says, "Ready, set . . . " and the team yells, "Go!" Can you think of more examples?

2. Today we're going to learn some call-and-response scripts to use in our classroom. The first one will be our signal to get quiet and focus on our learning. The second script will be to perk us up and generate some energy.

3. Okay. Let's practice our scripts.

(continued)

(continued)

FOLLOW-UP

Practice your scripts frequently until everybody knows them. Later, invite students to create new call-and-response cues. If they create several, put them in a hat and draw one out to use each month. Limit the number you use during a given time period and don't change them too often; otherwise, students may forget them.

VARIATIONS

Add motions to your scripts or try nonverbal scripts that use rhythms or sounds. For example:

> T: Clap, clap . . .
>
> S: Clap, clap, clap
>
> T: Stomp, stomp . . .
>
> S: Stomp, stomp, stomp

40. CRAZY QUIZ

☆ **PURPOSE**: establishing classroom rules and routines   ☆ **AGES**: 5-18

☆ **TIME**: 10-20 minutes, depending on number and age of students

☆ **MATERIALS**: LCD projector and screen, interactive whiteboard, or overhead projector

PREPARATION

Create a multiple-choice quiz on classroom etiquette and procedures (bathroom visits, arriving to class late, returning to class after an absence, turning in homework, and so on). If you have discussed specific rules and procedures with your students, make your questions specific. Otherwise, use general questions. This is a fun way to review the rules without creating a teacher-versus-student atmosphere.

Following are some sample questions.

1 **If you come to class tardy, you should:**

   a. Give the teacher a high five and holler "Yo!" to all of your friends.

   b. Hold a book in front of your face and sneak in.

   c Hand the teacher your hall pass and quietly sit down.

2 **How should we turn in homework?**

   a. Hand it to the teacher.

   b. Fold it into a paper airplane and fly it at the teacher.

   c Rub some grape jelly on it to make it look special.

   d. Stick it in your pocket to give it that nice wrinkled look.

3. **What should I do during tests?**

   a. Copy from the person beside me.

   b. Tap my feet constantly.

   c Drum my pencil on my desktop.

   d. Whistle under my breath.

   e. Grab my head and moan loudly.

   f. Quietly do my best.

(continued)

CRAZY QUIZ

(continued)

For younger students, create very simple questions with extremely silly answers, such as:

Where do we keep the crayons?

a. In our shoes

b. In the supply box

INSTRUCTIONS FOR STUDENTS

1 We're going to take a quiz about our classroom rules and procedures—but this isn't a normal quiz. So put on your thinking caps.

2 Here's question number one. *[Display the question.]* Who would like to read out the question and all the answers? *[Choose a volunteer or read it yourself.]*

FOLLOW-UP

Invite students to create their own crazy questions and use them to create a follow-up quiz.

VARIATION

If you don't have a projector, make copies of your Crazy Quiz for students. Give them a time limit to complete the quiz, then review it together.

41. CLEANUP TIME

☆ **PURPOSE:** establishing classroom rules and routines   ☆ **AGES:** 5-18

☆ **TIME:** 5-10 minutes, depending on number and age of students

☆ **MATERIALS:** audio recording: short segment of easily recognizable music

PREPARATION

Choose a song that is unique and easily recognizable. Record a section between 30 seconds and 2 minutes long. Make sure that your music is long enough to allow students to accomplish their cleanup tasks, but short enough to give a sense of urgency.

One art teacher I know uses the beginning of Beethoven's Fifth Symphony (the famous DAH-DAH-DAH-dah).

During your first class meeting, give students a short assignment that involves using art materials, reference books, dictionaries, or other classroom supplies. When you are ready to transition to the next activity, play your cleanup music.

INSTRUCTIONS FOR STUDENTS

1 Whenever you hear this: *[play the cleanup music again]* it means you have ___ seconds (or minutes) to stop what you are doing, clean up your work area, and put away any classroom materials you have been using.

2 Let's give it a try. I'm going to play it again and see if you can get everything cleaned up and be in your seat, ready to work, before the song is finished. *[Play the cleanup song.]*

FOLLOW-UP

Thank your students for cleaning up so quickly. If they finished before the song ended, lead them in a round of applause. If they didn't quite finish, thank them for giving it a good try. Give them another chance later in the class. Use this same cue throughout the school year whenever you want students to clean up and get ready to work. Don't change this song for variety's sake—this is one time when you want to maintain a steady routine.

VARIATIONS

Create different musical cues for various classroom activities: 5-10 minutes for Do Now (the task you want students to begin as soon as they enter your classroom); 10-15 minutes of instrumentals to play during journal writing; classical music for exams. When the music stops, it's time for students to stop what they are doing and get ready for the next activity.

42. GIVE ME THREE

☆ **PURPOSE:** establishing classroom rules and routines   ☆ **AGES:** 5–11

☆ **TIME:** 5–10 minutes, depending on number and age of students

☆ **MATERIALS:** poster board, bold marker, age-appropriate illustrations

PREPARATION

Choose three common behaviors that you want to reinforce in your classroom. Choose specific behaviors such as *Eyes on the Speaker* or *Listening Quietly*, as opposed to general concepts such as *Do Your Best*.

    Create a chart that lists your three behaviors, printed in large enough letters that they can be read easily from the back of the room. Include the number for each behavior. Use drawings or symbols to illustrate each element (such as a big eye, an oversized ear, or an animal with giant ears).

INSTRUCTIONS FOR STUDENTS

1. I'd like to discuss something important with you called Give Me Three—these three things will help me do my best teaching and help you do your best learning.

2. Number 1 is _____. This is important because _____.

3. Number 2 is _____. This is important because _____.

4. And number 3 is _____. We need to do this because _____.

5. Thank you very much for listening so nicely. As we go along, if I need to remind you of one of these three important behaviors, I'll just say the number. That way, we won't waste any time.

FOLLOW-UP

Include at least a brief explanation for each element of your chart. Even young students prefer rules that are based on logic.

    Then immediately begin using your chart, referring by number to the behavior you want to see. If you are giving instructions and somebody is chatting to a friend, simply say, "Jeremy, number 3, please." Continue with your instruction, pausing only to say "Thank you" when Jeremy complies. (In most cases, students will comply because being reminded by number feels more like guidance than a reprimand.)

VARIATIONS

Add one or two more elements (such as keep your hands to yourself) for Give Me Four or Give Me Five. Limit your list. More than five items will dilute their importance. Revise language and rules to use this activity with older students.

43. NOISE-O-METER

☆ *PURPOSE*: establishing classroom rules and routines   ☆ *AGES*: 5–18

☆ *TIME*: 10–30 minutes, depending on number and age of students

☆ *MATERIALS*: noise-o-meter

PREPARATION

Create a noise-o-meter for your classroom to suit the age and maturity of your students. Popular noise-o-meter models follow the design of car speedometers, red-yellow-green traffic lights, and round clock-style faces with an arrow that can be adjusted to point to the current level.

The following instructions will need to be modified to suit your categories and specific model. Very young students, for example, respond best to three simple categories: (1) no talking, (2) whisper, and (3) indoor voices.

(continued)

(continued)

INSTRUCTIONS FOR STUDENTS

1 In order to have the best learning environment, it's important for us to monitor the volume of our voices. So, we will be using this noise-o-meter as a guide. *[Show your noise-o-meter to the class.]*

2 We have four levels:

Level 1, Quiet Time, means no talking, please.

Level 2, On Your Own, means you should whisper. Please use this level when you are working independently but you need to ask somebody, including me, a question.

[For young students, model the behavior by whispering the words "whisper, please." Ask them to show you how well they can whisper.]

Level 3, Soft Voices, is for working with a partner or group.

Level 4, Indoor Voices, applies when we are talking all together as a class and you need to speak up so everybody can hear you.

FOLLOW-UP

Conduct an Internet search for "noise-o-meter" and you will find many posts by teachers describing their meters and how they introduce and implement them. Anecdotal evidence suggests that this is a very effective tool for all ages. Websites change frequently, but this one from the U.K. has many samples, some with illustrations: *www.primaryresources.co.uk/behaviour/behaviour.htm.*

VARIATION

Appoint a student noise monitor to gently remind classmates if they forget the current noise level. Rotate this job so everybody has a turn at being the monitor; this avoids the "traffic cop" mentality and reinforces the idea that all students are responsible for maintaining an orderly classroom where mutual respect is the norm.

NOISE-O-METER

44. MY KIND OF CLASS

☆ **PURPOSE**: establishing classroom rules and routines

☆ **AGES**: 7-adult

☆ **TIME**: 10-30 minutes, depending on number and age of students

☆ **MATERIALS**: template for students, pen or pencils

PREPARATION

Make a template with two numbered lists, each labeled from 1 through 10. Label the first list Things I Would Like to Do in This Class and the second list What I Would Like the Students in This Class to Do.

Greet students at the door. Invite them to choose seats or find their assigned seats (see *Find Your Folder* or *Symbol Search* in Chapter Three for quick ways to assign seats).

Give instructions *before* you distribute the templates. People stop listening when you give them something to read.

INSTRUCTIONS FOR STUDENTS

1. In a moment I'm going to give you a template I made for this class. On the template there are two lists. *[Hold up a sample template.]*

2. In the first list, I'd like you to write the things you would like to do in this class, such as research, reading on your own, or building models—whatever you enjoy.

3. For the second list, I would like to know what kind of behavior you would like to see from the students in this class. What would you like them to do to make this a comfortable classroom for you to learn in?

4. We're going to take __ minutes to fill out the templates. Then we'll discuss them together and see what we have. *[Now distribute your templates.]*

FOLLOW-UP

Ask volunteers to share items from their lists. Together, create a Classroom Code of Conduct or a set of Classroom Bylaws that everybody agrees will promote harmony and learning. Some teachers create a poster and ask students to sign it, à la Declaration of Independence. (Make sure you ask if there are any objections during your discussion, because you are going to ask them to sign the final document they create.)

If you have a "tough" class, ignore those who don't participate, provided they don't disrupt. If they do disrupt, tell them disrespect isn't tolerated in your classroom. Do what you have to do to remove them so the class can proceed with this important activity.

VARIATIONS

Instead of a printed template, ask students to step up and write their ideas on the board. Discuss each list separately. Or ask students to create a poster listing their Code of Conduct or Classroom Bylaws.

45. RULES BINGO

⭐ **PURPOSE:** establishing classroom rules and routines   ⭐ **AGES:** 6-16

⭐ **TIME:** 10-30 minutes, depending on number and age of students

⭐ **MATERIALS:** bingo cards, markers or chips, small prizes

PREPARATION

Make bingo cards with 9-25 squares per card. In each square, print a classroom rule such as Always Do Your Best, No Cell Phones in Class, or Use Your Indoor Voice. If humor is appropriate for your group, add one or two "goofy rules" such as No Giraffes in Class. Write each rule on a slip of paper and put all the slips into a box, bag, or jar. Make extra slips for each rule that appears more than once on the cards.

If you plan to use the bingo cards just once, distribute markers to students. If you plan to reuse the cards, hand out pennies, beans, poker chips, or construction paper dots.

Buy or make prizes (such as stickers, pencils, pipe cleaner animals, or balloons). Have enough prizes for the first few winners or one for every student.

Greet students at the door. Invite them to choose seats or find their assigned seats (see *Find Your Folder* or *Symbol Search* in Chapter Three for quick ways to assign seats).

Present your instructions before you distribute the cards and markers or chips.

INSTRUCTIONS FOR STUDENTS

1. In a moment I'm going to give you a bingo card that has some of our classroom rules printed on it *[hold up a sample card]* and a marker (or some chips).

2. Then I'll ask for volunteers to take turns drawing a rule from the bag (or jar). If you have that rule on your card, draw an X (or place a marker) on it.

3. When you have one complete line filled in on your card, say "Bingo!" and I will give you your prize.

4. Let's begin. *[Now distribute your cards and markers.]*

FOLLOW-UP

Repeat this activity a few times during the first week of school as a fun way to review the classroom rules.

VARIATIONS

To make the game more challenging, require students to fill in an X, a cross, the center square and all four corners, or all of the squares on their cards before they can call "Bingo."

Taken from *Kick-Start Your Class: Academic Icebreakers to Engage Students.* Copyright © 2012 by LouAnne Johnson. Reproduced by permission of Jossey-Bass, an Imprint of Wiley. www.josseybass.com.

46. SEAT SCRAMBLE SIGNAL

☆ **PURPOSE:** establishing classroom rules and routines

☆ **AGES:** 5-18

☆ **TIME:** 2-10 minutes, depending on number and age of students

☆ **MATERIALS:** brief recorded music segments, posters and photos, rewards (optional)

PREPARATION

Record 15-, 30-, and 60-second segments of a unique, easily identifiable song. Post several interesting, amusing, and thought-provoking posters and photographs on the walls of your classroom.

After students arrive and are seated, introduce yourself, then give your instructions.

INSTRUCTIONS FOR STUDENTS

1. I like to have a friendly, comfortable classroom, and I don't like shouting at people. I'm sure you don't enjoy having people shout at you, either. And I would like for us to get our work done and have fun, instead of wasting time.

2. So when you are working independently and I need everybody to quickly take their seats, I am going to play this song. *[Play one of your recorded segments.]*

3. That's our Seat Scramble Signal. Whenever you hear that song, you will have __ seconds to sit down in your seat, stop talking, and be prepared to listen.

4. Since everybody is seated right now, we can't practice. So I'd like you to get up and walk around and take a look at the posters and photos on the walls. Feel free to discuss them with your classmates if you like. *[Instead of viewing artwork, you might choose a different icebreaker that involves students moving around and talking to each other. Use your Seat Scramble Signal to indicate the end of that activity.]*

Give students 5–6 minutes to mingle and view the artwork, then give the Seat Scramble Signal. Praise them for their efforts—even if they don't quite make it to their seats before the music ends. If they do get to their seats, distribute rewards (such as pencils, erasers, or stickers) if you choose. If they don't make it, practice again.

FOLLOW-UP

Repeat the Seat Scramble Signal frequently, so it becomes a habit for students to quickly take their seats whenever they hear it. After a few weeks, challenge them, if appropriate, by using a shorter segment.

SEAT SCRAMBLE SIGNAL

47. WE'RE GOING READING

⭐ **PURPOSE**: establishing classroom rules and routines ⭐ **AGES**: 4–8

⭐ **TIME**: 5–10 minutes, depending on number and age of students

⭐ **MATERIALS**: reading rug, floor pillows or mats, reading tree (optional)

PREPARATION

Create a fun, comfortable area in your classroom just for reading. If possible, provide incandescent or natural daylight in this area instead of fluorescent lights, which can cause vision problems. *(See Chapter Eight in* Teaching Outside the Box *[Jossey-Bass, 2011] to learn about the connection between light and learning.)* Arrange floor pillows, mats, or a special reading rug with squares or letters. If you assign reading seats, rotate them periodically so everybody has a chance to sit near the teacher.

Create a reading mascot and make a poster of your mascot to display. (We'll use Rufus the Reading Rabbit as an example).

Optional: Place a real or fake palm tree in the reading area or create a paper tree and let each student print his and her name on a leaf and glue it to the tree.

INSTRUCTIONS FOR STUDENTS

1 In a moment we're going to move over to our reading area for a special story. But first, we need to learn our reading song. It goes like this:

   We're going reading, yes we are. Reading can take us near or far. We can go to ___ *[name of a local town]* or Timbuktu. Rufus loves reading, and we do, too.

2 Now let's practice our song twice in our seats. Then we'll all stand up and I will lead the way to the reading area while we sing.

Practice your song. Then lead your class around the room, marching and singing, and make your way to the reading area.

FOLLOW-UP

If students can write, have them copy the words to the reading song on a piece of paper. Or let them draw a map to the reading area or a reading-related picture.

VARIATIONS

Draw student names from a bag to select the Reading Captain to lead the way to the reading area for each visit. Select another captain to lead students back to their desks (or play your Seat Scramble Signal, presented earlier in this chapter).

48. YOU & ME PACT

⭐ **PURPOSE:** establishing classroom rules and routines   ⭐ **AGES:** 7–17

⭐ **TIME:** 10–30 minutes, depending on number and age of students

⭐ **MATERIALS:** template for students, pens or pencils

PREPARATION

Divide a sheet of paper into two equal halves—label one half Me and the other half You. Create 5–10 blank lines on each half. Make enough copies for all the students in your class.

Create a handout with a brief but challenging assignment for students to do independently after they finish the activity. Make copies and place them on your desk.

Greet students at the door. Hand each student a template and invite them to choose seats or find their assigned seats (*see Chapter Three for quick ways to assign seats*).

Introduce yourself, then begin your instructions.

(continued)

(continued)

INSTRUCTIONS FOR STUDENTS

1. On the "You" half of your sheet, please list 5-10 things that you would like me to do to help you learn or to create a comfortable classroom for you.

2. On the "Me" half of your sheet, please list 5-10 things that you can do to create the best learning opportunity for yourself.

3. Your list is private—you don't have to show it to anybody but me. We'll discuss your list to make sure we both understand and agree with it. Then we'll both sign it to create a You & Me Pact that will help us work together.

4. Please raise your hand when you are finished and I'll get to you as soon as I can. After your pact is signed, please take a copy of the handout on my desk and begin working on the assignment.

FOLLOW-UP

Circulate the room to offer feedback and encouragement. As each student finishes, read his or her list. If it's acceptable, sign your name on it. Initial any changes that need to be made. Ask the student to sign it. Collect the signed pacts and make copies so you and every student have a copy of each individual pact.

VARIATION

Create one pact for the entire class. Ask students to write their ideas on the board. Discuss each item and vote whether to include it in the pact for your room. Ask students to create a poster to display your You & Me Pact.

YOU & ME PACT

Chapter Five

Teamwork: Building Classroom Communities

The activities in this chapter promote laughter, interaction, conversation, and sharing. Although there is a slight element of competition in some of them, winning or losing is not the focus. Rather than defeating an opposing team, the focus here is on working together to accomplish a goal or meet a challenge. In the process, bonds are forged among students and between the students and the teacher.

When students enjoy a sense of classroom community, they behave better, cooperate more willingly, and earn better grades. Community-building icebreakers take advantage of the natural desire of people, especially adolescents, to socialize via structured activities that have a positive focus and a purpose.

Laughter is Good for the Brain and the Heart

Scientific research proves that laughter creates positive brain chemicals—endorphins—similar to those that runners and other athletes experience. Group laughter not only creates endorphins, but it also promotes bonding between the people who laugh together. That is one of the reasons why so many public speakers begin with a joke. Even if the joke isn't particularly funny, most people will laugh in an effort to be polite. And laughing together bonds them.

Teachers can use their knowledge of brain science to disarm potential disrupters in our classrooms. It's difficult for students to hate somebody who makes them laugh. And even if they don't laugh out loud, just being among laughing people can reduce their anxiety and stress levels.

49. FIND THE TEACHER

☆ **PURPOSE:** teamwork: building classroom communities   ☆ **AGES:** 5–adult

☆ **TIME:** 5–10 minutes

☆ **MATERIALS:** photographs of the teacher as an elementary school student

PREPARATION

Find a class photo from your own school days that shows several students, including you. Or create a collage of photos of classmates from your elementary school days, including one photo of yourself.

Create a template titled What Do You Think? with three blank lines numbered 1–3.

Assign students to work in pairs or teams (*see Chapter Three for some quick and easy methods of assigning pairs and teams*).

INSTRUCTIONS FOR STUDENTS

1 In a moment I'm going to give each pair (or team) a photo (or collage). These are not current photographs. These are from my own school days. Your mission is to see if you can correctly identify me from among the students in the photos.

2 After you locate my picture, your next task is to make a list of three things:

→ What do you think was my favorite after-school snack?

→ What do you think was my favorite school subject?

→ What do you think I wanted to be when I grew up? *[Distribute photos and templates.]*

3. When you believe you have found me, and after you have made your list, raise your hand and I will come and see how well you have done your detective work.

FOLLOW-UP

Ask for student feedback on the activity. Guide the discussion to the topic of dreams for the future. Ask younger students to consider their own dreams and what steps they can take to make those dreams a reality. If students are adults, ask them to share their own childhood dreams with the class or with a partner.

VARIATIONS

If you have several photos from your childhood, you can create multiple collages instead of giving the same one to each team.

Ask students to identify how modern clothing, hairstyles, school buildings, and rooms differ from the ones shown in the picture. This can lead to a lively discussion of culture, trends, and history.

50. TEAM CLASSROOM CONCENTRATION

☆ **PURPOSE**: teamwork: building classroom communities　　☆ **AGES**: 5-18

☆ **TIME**: 10-20 minutes, depending on number and complexity of cards

☆ **MATERIALS**: custom card sets featuring letters, words, or pictures; pairs of dice

PREPARATION

Create an age-appropriate set of 5-20 cards containing words and/or pictures of people, animals, or objects. For older students, create cards with facts or subject-specific vocabulary terms (such as "spiders are arachnids," Pythagorean theorem, or onomatopoeia). Copy all the cards to make a deck consisting of matched pairs. Then make enough copies of the entire deck to distribute one deck to each student pair or team.

Divide students into pairs or three-member teams (*see Chapter Three for some quick and easy methods of assigning pairs and teams*). Give each pair or team a pair of dice.

INSTRUCTIONS FOR STUDENTS

1. I'm going to give each pair (or group) a deck of cards. When you get your deck, place all the cards on your desk, facedown, in rows, without looking at them. No peeking. That spoils the mystery. *[For students who need a visual model, demonstrate how to lay out the cards.]*

2. To win Classroom Concentration, you must match up all your cards. When it's your turn, choose a card and turn it faceup. Then choose another card and turn it faceup. If your two cards don't match, turn them back over so they are facedown. If your cards match, take that pair and set it aside. Don't shift the remaining cards around—leave them where they are so you can remember their locations.

3. The next person turns over any card and then tries to find its match. It may take a few turns before somebody makes a match, but it gets easier as you go along.

4. To see who goes first in your group, roll the dice one time. The person with the lowest number goes first.

5. After __ minutes, I will give you the signal to stop. We'll count how many matches you have.

(continued)

(continued)

FOLLOW-UP

When students finish their lessons early, let them play the game quietly in an area where they won't bother students who are still working.

VARIATION

Working in pairs, let students design and create their own card pairs using information from their books or that they have studied in class. Let them swap decks and play each other's games as a fun way to review what they have learned.

51. FIRST-DAY FEELINGS

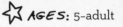 ☆ **PURPOSE**: teamwork: building classroom communities ☆ **AGES**: 5-adult

☆ **TIME**: 5-15 minutes

☆ **MATERIALS**: chalkboard and chalk; or whiteboard or paper and markers

PREPARATION

Arrange desks or chairs so that all students can easily see the board. A chalkboard or whiteboard is best, but if those are not available, a large sheet of paper can be taped to the wall for this activity. Provide plenty of markers and make them easily accessible to students.

INSTRUCTIONS FOR STUDENTS

1. The first day of school can be both exciting and scary, and most of us have many different feelings about starting a new class or a new term. We may be excited about learning new information and skills, but we may also be worried about many things as well. I'd like us to take a moment now to think about what we are feeling. *[Allow 30-60 seconds for reflection.]*

2. Now I'd like to invite you to come up to the board and write down anything that is on your mind about school—things you are worried about and things you are excited about. This won't be graded, and you don't have to participate. But I would appreciate it very much if you shared your feelings with the class.

3. I'll start by writing two things that I am thinking about right now. *[Write two comments, such as: "All those tests! Who will be in my class? How will I remember everything?"]*

FOLLOW-UP

Allow a bit of time for students to muster their courage and step forward. Encourage them by moving around the room and asking individual students what they are thinking or feeling. Invite them personally to write their comments on the board.

After students have filled the board or paper, take a few moments to sit and look at the comments. Then ask students for feedback on the activity. Are there any common worries? Do they have suggestions for helping classmates cope with various stressors or problems? This activity could also be used as a journal prompt about first-day feelings.

VARIATIONS

Instead of doing this as a whole-group activity, assign students to work in pairs or teams to come up with individual lists of first-day feelings and concerns. Then ask the pairs or groups to share their lists with the class. Young students can do this activity orally and share their concerns in small groups or pairs.

(continued)

FIRST-DAY FEELINGS

(continued)

i can't SPEL 2 GOOD ⸛

in the Bathroom
Sex + drugs

TESTS

BAD HAIR

homework

I'm
HUNGRY

Boys

BULLIES

getting
LOST

Math

the MEAN girls

B.O.

Where's the bathroom?

gym class

WILL the teacher like me?

Will I like the teacher?

Who will I EAT LUNCH WITH?

REPORT
CARDS

biology

zits

getting dressed for p.e.

the wrong shoes

Will I have any friends?

Sample First-Day Feelings List

52. FINISH THE STORY

☆ **PURPOSE:** teamwork: building classroom communities

☆ **AGES:** 5–adult

☆ **TIME:** 10–20 minutes

☆ **MATERIALS:** story starters (see Preparation section)

PREPARATION

Create an age-appropriate first paragraph for a story that involves at least two main characters (human or animal). Write your own or copy a brief selection from a book. Make copies of your first paragraph so you have one copy for each pair or team of students.

Prepare index cards with a variety of cues, such as An Argument, A Discovery, A Problem, A Big Mistake, A Dangerous Adventure, A Big Surprise, and so on.

Assign students to work in pairs or teams (*see Chapter Three for some quick and easy methods of assigning pairs and teams*). Give each pair or team your story starter.

INSTRUCTIONS FOR STUDENTS

1. Everybody has the first paragraph of a story. Your mission is to finish the story. But don't worry, you don't have to write it all—just one or two paragraphs.

2. I'm going to come around and give each pair or team a card that has a cue for what happens next. Your job is to write that part of the story. Then we will put them all together and see what we have. *[Distribute your cue cards.]*

3. You will have 10 minutes to write your section. Don't worry about spelling or grammar. Just get the story down on paper (and keep it clean). We can always correct our mistakes later.

FOLLOW-UP

Randomly assign a number, beginning with number 1, to each pair or team to indicate the order that they will be asked to share their story section. Read your story start, then ask students to read their sections.

Note: Do not force students to read aloud if they are reluctant—this can make reading a negative activity, and brain research shows that we store emotional memories along with information. Instead, ask for volunteers from the class to read their sections or read them yourself. This activity is meant to be fun.

VARIATIONS

Type your students' stories and make copies to use later. Add more chapters or an ending. Ask students to illustrate the story and create a handwritten book, or scan student illustrations and use desktop publishing to create a "published" version. If possible, let them do all the editing and publishing as a class project. Make copies for parents.

53. JUGGLING TEAMS

☆ **PURPOSE**: teamwork: building classroom communities

☆ **TIME**: 5–15 minutes

☆ **MATERIALS**: soft balls or beanbags

☆ **AGES**: 5–adult

PREPARATION

Arrange desks or chairs or locate a space outside the classroom where students can move about freely.

Assign students to work in pairs or teams (*see Chapter Three for some quick and easy methods of assigning pairs and teams*). Provide each team with one set of beanbags or balls.

Before you begin the activity, ask if there are any students in class who know how to juggle. If so, invite them to give a quick demonstration. If not, show a short instructional video such as those available on YouTube or SchoolTube. Here's one sample: *www.schooltube.com/video/726304733abb4afd8e62/Juggling-basics-LA-Youth.*

If your school blocks Internet access, download a video to your cell phone or other electronic device or check out a DVD from your local library.

Also, before you begin, demonstrate your Attention Getter to indicate that you need students to stop what they are doing and quietly pay attention. (See the Introduction for details.)

INSTRUCTIONS FOR STUDENTS

1 Your mission is to practice tossing your beanbag or ball softly to your partner, keeping as many bags or balls in motion as you can.

2 Don't worry if you aren't perfect jugglers. We all make mistakes. The important thing is to learn from them and make improvements. Ready, set, go.

FOLLOW-UP

Ask students to share their feedback about the activity. What did they learn? How did they adjust their movements to improve their juggling? What mathematical or physics principles can they see in the art of juggling (for example, speed, arc, or relative motion)?

Invite students to share other skills or talents they have that are not part of the normal school curriculum. Create a calendar, and schedule regular student demonstrations throughout the school term. After each demonstration, conduct research about the particular skill involved—its history, cultural connections, performance or competition aspects, and methods of instruction.

54. OUR CLASS PUZZLE

☆ **PURPOSE:** teamwork: building classroom communities

☆ **TIME:** 10–20 minutes

☆ **MATERIALS:** poster board, razor knife, markers (optional)

☆ **AGES:** 5–adult

PREPARATION

Draw a colorful design on a sheet of poster board or attach a ready-made poster(s) or photograph(s) to cover the entire sheet. On the back of the board, draw pencil lines to indicate where you will cut the board, making sure you create as many pieces as there are student names on your roster. (Create a couple of extra pieces for unexpected arrivals.) Then, using a razor knife, cut your poster into a jigsaw puzzle.

Create a space on a table or the floor where students will have room to move around and assemble the puzzle.

Greet students at the door as they enter your classroom. Hand each student a puzzle piece and ask them to be seated and wait for instructions. (If you have extra pieces, distribute them randomly.)

INSTRUCTIONS FOR STUDENTS

1 Each of you is holding one piece of our class jigsaw puzzle. Your mission now is to assemble the puzzle as quickly as possible to discover what it looks like.

2 After our puzzle is assembled, we'll tape it together and display it on the wall.

(continued)

FOLLOW-UP

Ask students to consider ways in which a jigsaw puzzle is like a group of students. During the discussion, mention that they are a learning community—when they join together, they create a new entity. If one piece is missing, the puzzle is not complete. Use this as a springboard for a discussion of how they can help one another succeed in school.

VARIATIONS

Instead of creating a design or picture for your puzzle, use a black marker to draw a series of lines and squiggles to indicate the back of the puzzle on a sheet of poster board. Then cut the board into puzzle pieces (enough to give each student a piece, along with a few extras). Give students 5-10 minutes to decorate their pieces with their names and whatever they choose to draw. (Keep it clean!) Then assemble the puzzle.

Another variation is to create four or more smaller puzzles (use different colored markers to indicate the backs of each separate puzzle to avoid confusion and to aid students in assembling them). Students with matching puzzle pieces form teams that will work together in the future.

OUR CLASS PUZZLE

55. MULTI-BALLOON FLOAT

☆ **PURPOSE:** teamwork: building classroom communities   ☆ **AGES:** 5–18

☆ **TIME:** 5–15 minutes, depending on age of students and number of balloons

☆ **MATERIALS:** balloons in various colors

PREPARATION

Find a location big enough for students to move around safely.

Group your balloons by color into sets of 3–6.

Before you begin the activity, demonstrate your start and stop signals so students can respond quickly when time is up or you want to give further instructions.

INSTRUCTIONS FOR STUDENTS

1 I'm going to give each person __ balloons to blow up and tie. When you are finished blowing up your balloons, you can help your neighbor or just wait quietly.

2 Now we need to spread out a bit. Make sure that you are not standing next to someone whose balloons are the same color as yours. We don't want to get confused.

3 When I give the start signal, we'll see how long you can keep all your balloons in the air. Ready, set, go.

After 1–2 minutes, give the stop signal. Then assign partners and give students another go at keeping their balloons afloat. Finally, give the go signal and let all the students work at keeping all the balloons afloat. Add more balloons, if necessary, to increase the challenge and motivation.

FOLLOW-UP

Ask for student feedback on the activity. Let this lead to a discussion of how much more we can accomplish when we work together.

VARIATION

Begin by giving one-third of the students in your class six balloons each. Give them a start signal and see how long they can keep all six afloat. Then assign partners from the students who have been watching and try again. Finally, add a third person to each pair and see how long they can keep all six (or more) balloons in the air.

56 PAPER TURNOVER

☆ **PURPOSE**: teamwork: building classroom communities ☆ **AGES**: 5–adult

☆ **TIME**: 10–15 minutes

☆ **MATERIALS**: large pieces of brown shipping paper, at least 48 in. × 48 in.

PREPARATION

Arrange desks or chairs or locate a space outside the classroom where students can move about freely.

Before beginning the activity, assign students to work as pairs or teams. (*See Chapter Three for some quick and easy methods of assigning pairs and teams.*) Give each team one sheet of shipping paper.

Demonstrate the Attention Getter you will use to indicate that time is up or that you need everybody's quiet attention for further instructions. (See the Introduction for details.)

INSTRUCTIONS FOR STUDENTS

1 Each team has a sheet of paper. Your first task is to place the paper on the floor and stand on the paper facing your partner(s).

2 Now your mission is to turn over the entire sheet of paper—without tearing the paper and without stepping off the paper onto the floor. If anybody steps onto the floor, your team will have to stop and start over again from the beginning.

3 You will have __ minutes to complete your turnover. Ready? Begin.

FOLLOW-UP

Ask for student feedback on the activity. Encourage discussion by asking open-ended questions that require reflection: How many teams accomplished their mission? How did they do it? Did one person in the group take charge? Were they able to cooperate in order to complete the task? Would it have been easier if the teacher had assigned a leader or captain for each group before they began the exercise?

Use this activity as a springboard for discussions about working together to accomplish a goal. Ask students to self-reflect about whether they prefer to be a leader or a follower. Point out that both are necessary—all leaders or all followers does not work.

VARIATIONS

Mix up the teams or pairs and try the activity again. Or ask students to design similar challenges for the class.

57. TEAM TRIVIA

☆ **PURPOSE:** teamwork: building classroom communities   ☆ **AGES:** 6-adult

☆ **TIME:** 10-20 minutes

☆ **MATERIALS:** age-appropriate trivia questions, small whiteboards or paper and markers

PREPARATION

Prepare a series of trivia questions about a specific academic subject or a mixture of topics such as popular culture, music, athletics, movies, science, history, politics, art, or literature. Include some very simple questions (to build confidence and inspire participation), some silly questions (laughter creates positive brain chemicals and promotes group bonding), and some very challenging questions (success at difficult tasks creates satisfaction and encourages internal motivation).

Create a number of award certificates or humorous trophies with citations such as Dynamite Discussers, Top-Notch Thinkers, Big Brains, and Incredible Intellectuals. Make as many certificates or trophies as you have teams, so that each team will receive recognition.

Divide your students into teams of 3-4 people. Group teams together in various locations of the classroom where everybody can easily see the whiteboard, chalkboard, or projector screen. As you play the game, display the questions as a visual aid to learners who do not process verbal instructions quickly.

Give each team an individual whiteboard and dry-erase marker or several sheets of paper and a bold marker.

INSTRUCTIONS FOR STUDENTS

1. I'm going to ask a series of trivia questions. You will have 60 seconds to discuss the question among your team and write your answer on your whiteboard or paper.

2. When I give the signal, hold up your team's answer so I can see if it is correct.

3. Do I have a volunteer to keep a running tally of the number of correct answers for each team? *[If two people volunteer, choose them both to work as a team. If nobody volunteers, do this yourself.]*

FOLLOW-UP

Ask 10 questions and judge student engagement or cooperation. If it's high, continue with another 10 questions. Then tally up the scores and award trophies or certificates to each team. Congratulate or acknowledge students for working together (even if not everybody did—the majority will, and they deserve recognition).

Invite students to create their own questions or awards for use in a future trivia contest. Use this as a community builder or as a learning tool such as a review for major tests or to summarize what students learned during a particular unit of study.

58. UNUSUAL MEASURES*

☆ **PURPOSE**: teamwork: building classroom communities

☆ **TIME**: 10–15 minutes

☆ **MATERIALS**: none required

☆ **AGES**: 5–adult

PREPARATION

Assign students to work as partners or teams (see Chapter Three for some quick and easy methods of assigning pairs and teams).

INSTRUCTIONS FOR STUDENTS

1 Your mission is to measure two different objects in this room, using two different and unusual measuring instruments, such as a stapler or a part of your body. For example, this desk might be 47 thumbs wide and the doorway might be 15 staplers tall.

2 You will have 10 minutes to complete your measurements. Then each team will share its findings with the rest of the class.

FOLLOW-UP

Invite each team to share its objects and measurements.

Ask for student feedback about this activity. How did they select their measuring devices? Would they recommend changing our standard measurements of inches, feet, and yards to something else? Why or why not?

VARIATION

Assign students specific large and small objects to measure, such as a textbook and a whiteboard or a computer monitor and a person.

*Source: Adapted from an activity in Eric Jensen's wonderful book Brain-Compatible Strategies (Corwin Press, 2004).

PART TWO
Sticking to the Subject

In this section of the book, we'll look at icebreakers targeted for specific academic subjects—math, science, language arts, reading, social studies, technology, art, music, and English language learners—although many of them can be used effectively in any classroom.

Attention, Please

Once again, I suggest that if you haven't yet read the Introduction to this book, you might read the section titled "Create an Attention Getter." These signals can be one of a teacher's best classroom management tools. They let students know you need everybody's quiet attention or that a specific period of time has passed without having to raise your voice or waste precious time. Attention Getters are especially useful during icebreakers or other activities in which students become so engaged and excited that they lose track of time.

Chapter Six
Mathematical Possibilities

Math is a scary subject for many students—and adults. For some reason, math seems to be the single most common stumbling block in education.

Many people decide early on during their school years that they "just don't get math" or that they are "math challenged." And once those beliefs are formed, they are very persistent. One reason that these negative feelings persist is that human brains store emotional memories along with information and skills. So when we retrieve information or practice skills, we recall the same emotions we felt during our learning episodes. Because so many students find their first math lessons difficult and frustrating, they develop an attitude about math that prevents them from realizing that they might actually enjoy math.

Math icebreakers can help relieve students' anxiety and create positive attitudes towards math by using numbers and mathematical knowledge in challenging and enjoyable activities that do not result in a pass-or-fail grade. Instead, they encourage thinking, problem solving, and social learning. Each new positive experience with math helps students overcome those old negative attitudes and memories.

59. BALANCING ACT

☆ **PURPOSE:** math icebreaker: symmetry   ☆ **AGES:** 7–15

☆ **TIME:** 10–20 minutes

☆ **MATERIALS:** paper and pencils or markers

PREPARATION

Create a slide show or a set of posters or display samples of objects or scenes that demonstrate the concept of symmetry. Place paper and pencils or markers where they are easily accessible to students.

Before you begin the activity, show the slides or discuss the posters or objects, asking students what they all have in common. Try to lead them to the idea of symmetry instead of telling them. After your brief discussion, write the word *Symmetry* on the board and explain the principle.

INSTRUCTIONS FOR STUDENTS

1 In a moment I'm going to ask you to get a sheet of paper and two or three markers of different colors. Your mission is to create your own symmetrical design, using at least two different colors and three different shapes.

2 If you aren't quite sure you understand symmetry, sketch your design lightly in pencil first. Then discuss your design with one or two classmates and get their opinions. If you still aren't sure, raise your hand and I will come and assist you.

3 After you have finished your symmetrical design, show it to me and then tack it to the board. When all the designs are posted, we will review them together.

FOLLOW-UP

Ask students to make lists of symmetrical designs that occur in nature. Find examples of objects in your classroom that contain symmetry.

VARIATIONS

Computers. If you have computers available, let students work alone or in teams to create symmetrical designs on the computer. Create a slide show of all the designs to review after they are finished.

Bodies. Assign students to work in pairs or in 4-person teams: their mission is to create a symmetrical design using just their bodies. Two people could face each other, one with left hand raised, one with right hand raised, and both looking up at the ceiling, creating a mirror image.

(continued)

Taken from *Kick-Start Your Class: Academic Icebreakers to Engage Students.* Copyright © 2012 by LouAnne Johnson. Reproduced by permission of Jossey-Bass, an Imprint of Wiley. www.josseybass.com.

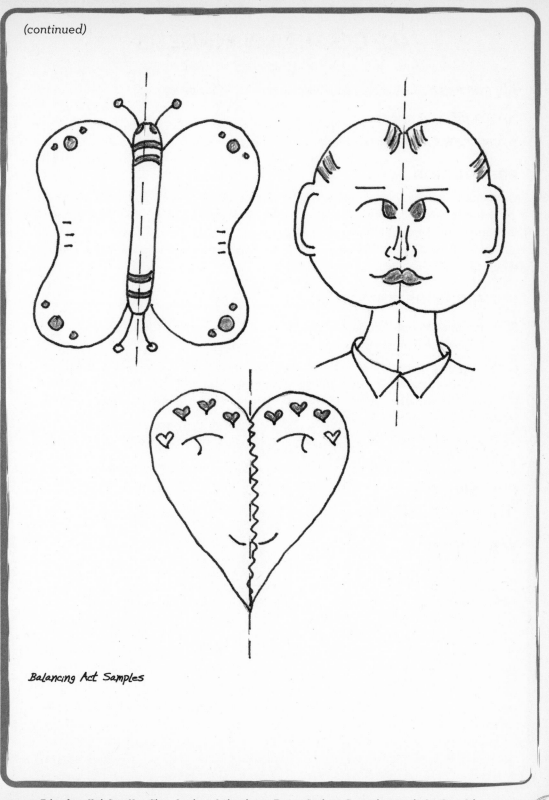

Balancing Act Samples

60. COUNT MY FINGERS

☆ **PURPOSE**: math icebreaker: counting   ☆ **AGES**: 4-7

☆ **TIME**: 5-10 minutes

☆ **MATERIALS**: collection of paper hands (optional)

PREPARATION

Optional: Create a series of ten large paper hands: two identical hands with one finger up, two with three fingers up, two with four up, and two with an open hand. (Technically, the thumb isn't a finger, but for counting purposes, an open hand is five fingers.)

Ask students to sit on the floor or in chairs, forming a semicircle around you where they can all see you clearly.

INSTRUCTIONS FOR STUDENTS

1 We're going to play Count My Fingers. Your job is to count to three: one, two, three. Let's practice that together: "one, two three." Excellent.

2 Now we're going to count and each time you get to three, I'm going to hold up one or two of my counting hands. [*Show students your paper hands. Hold up each hand separately and ask students to count the fingers. Then hold up two paper hands and ask them to count the fingers.*]

3 Ready to play? Let's count, "one, two, three." [*Hold up one or two hands.*] Count my fingers. How many do you see?

FOLLOW-UP

Let students take turns holding the paper hands up for classmates to count.

VARIATIONS

Instead of letting students shout out the number of fingers they see, ask them to raise their hands and call on them to answer. Or simply go around the room, calling on a different child each time. Call on each student twice before you end the game.

61. MATCHSTICK PUZZLES

⭐ **PURPOSE:** math icebreaker: brain teaser   ⭐ **AGES:** 7–adult

⭐ **TIME:** 10–20 minutes

⭐ **MATERIALS:** matchstick puzzles (available from books or the Internet), matchsticks

PREPARATION

Find a selection of age-appropriate matchstick puzzles of varying degrees of difficulty (students may surprise you by having more or less ability to solve them than you expected).

In various locations around the classroom, create individual puzzle displays: post a copy of the puzzle (enlarge it, if possible, or copy it onto a poster so it will be easily visible). Lay out matchsticks in the puzzle format on a counter, table, or desktop. Provide extra matchsticks for students to manipulate. Number the displays 1, 2, 3, and so on to identify them.

Divide students into pairs or teams (see Chapter Three for quick and easy ways to assign partners or teams). Give each pair a starting number that will correspond to the puzzle displays. This works best if you create enough individual puzzle displays so that no more than two teams will be starting at any one station at the same time.

INSTRUCTIONS FOR STUDENTS

1. When I give the signal to begin, your mission is to find the puzzle station that matches your starting number. Work together to solve the puzzle at your station.

2. When you have solved the puzzle, raise your hand to let me know. Then move on to a different station—try to choose a station where there aren't too many people.

3. Feel free to help your classmates if they get stuck. But don't just do the puzzle for them; make suggestions to help them solve it themselves.

FOLLOW-UP

Ask for student feedback on the puzzle activity. Some students may find it very frustrating. Discuss as a class what skills are involved in solving these puzzles. Ask students to share their own tactics for solving them. Reassure those who can't do them that they aren't stupid. Let this discussion lead to the topic of multiple intelligences (musical, verbal, spatial, and so on). We are all smart in our own ways.

Ask students to work alone or with partners to create their own matchstick puzzles to challenge the class.

VARIATION

Make copies of the puzzles and provide students with matchsticks so they can lay out the sticks on their own desks and work with them.

MATCHSTICK PUZZLES

62. THE NUMBER GAME

☆ **PURPOSE**: math icebreaker: getting acquainted

☆ **TIME**: 10–20 minutes

☆ **MATERIALS**: templates and pencils

☆ **AGES**: 5–adult

PREPARATION

Create a list of phrases that all begin with a number: Seven Days in a Week, The Three Musketeers, 101 Dalmatians, Twenty-Four Hours in a Day, Twelve Months in a Year, Twelve Eggs in a Dozen, Twenty-Six Letters in the Alphabet, Sixty Seconds in a Minute, 52 Weeks in a Year, Four Quarts in a Gallon, and so on. For younger students, make the list simpler, with familiar characters and numbers from popular stories such as "Goldilocks and the Three Bears."

Create a template that lists the numbers and the first letter of the following words. Using the examples just given, we would have this list:

→ 7 D in a W

→ The 3 M

→ 101 D

→ 24 H in a D

→ 12 M in a Y

→ 12 E in a D

→ 26 L in the A

→ 60 S in a M

→ 52 W in a Y

→ 4 Q in a G

Distribute the templates to students and then give the instructions and pencils.

(continued)

THE NUMBER GAME

(continued)

INSTRUCTIONS FOR STUDENTS

1 On your template you will see a list of things that begin with a number and the initials for a phrase that goes with the number. Let's look at the first one. It says "7 D in a W." Can anybody guess what that represents? *[If nobody can guess, don't tell them. Give them gentle hints, such as "What could D in a W mean? Dogs in a Warehouse? Ducks in a Wading Pool?" If necessary, offer a second example.]*

2 You will have __ minutes to see how many you can fill in. Then we'll review them as a class. The pencils are yours to keep as a welcome gift.

FOLLOW-UP

Ask students to create their own templates for classmates to fill in.

VARIATION

If time is an issue, create a few different templates, each with 5 items in the list. Complete one list each day for the first week of class as an opening activity.

THE NUMBER GAME

63. PEOPLE SHAPES

☆ **PURPOSE**: math icebreaker: geometric shapes    ☆ **AGES**: 7–adult

☆ **TIME**: 10–20 minutes

☆ **MATERIALS**: precut pieces of rope or twine

PREPARATION

Create large posters showing different geometric shapes that have equal sides: square, equilateral triangle, pentagon, and hexagon.

Precut rope or twine into 22-foot segments. Make enough segments to distribute one segment to each team when your class is divided into 4-person teams.

Divide students into 4-person teams. If you have an uneven number, create one or two 3-person teams (see Chapter Three for quick and easy ways to assign teams). Assign teams yourself, instead of asking students to form them, to avoid having a student accidentally (or intentionally) left out.

INSTRUCTIONS FOR STUDENTS

1 In a moment I'm going to give each team a section of rope. Your job is to use the rope to create the largest possible square (or equilateral triangle or pentagon or hexagon). You will have __ minutes. Here's the signal I will use to let you know the time is up. *[Demonstrate your Attention Getter—see the Introduction for details.]*

2 You may or may not be able to use the entire rope to create your shape. You will have to figure out a way to measure it without using a ruler or tape measure.

3. Ready? Begin.

FOLLOW-UP

Measure the finished shapes. Ask each team to share the methods they used to create equal lengths of rope.

Repeat the activity with a more challenging shape. Or give each team a different shape to create during the time limit.

VARIATIONS

For older students, increase the challenge by assigning teams whose task is to create the largest possible 3-dimensional square using a precut length of rope within a specific time limit. Or cut twine into 22-inch segments and let students work alone.

64. RHYTHM & WORDS

☆ **PURPOSE**: math icebreaker   ☆ **AGES**: 5–18

☆ **TIME**: 10–15 minutes

☆ **MATERIALS**: whiteboard or chalkboard or easel paper and markers

PREPARATION

Create lists of 1-, 2-, 3-, and 4-syllable words where the accent is on the first syllable—for example, *alligator, hummingbird, donkey*, and *fish*, or *Wonder Woman, Spider Man, Nemo*, and *Shrek*. Keep your list on hand. If necessary, you can supply the words for the first round. With practice, students will quickly catch on.

Make four columns on your board titled *4-Syllable, 3-Syllable, 2-Syllable*, and *1-Syllable*. Write one or two sample words under each column.

INSTRUCTIONS FOR STUDENTS

1 We're going to think about the rhythm of words. First, let's make a list of 1-syllable words. *[For young students, skip this step and use your list. As students suggest words, print them in the appropriate columns. If their suggestions don't have first-syllable accents, ask them to think of alternates. Repeat for all columns.]*

2 Now we're going to play out our words, but first, I need a volunteer who can keep the rhythm, like a bass drum—boom, boom, boom—keeping a regular beat, without speeding up or slowing down while the rest of us tap out the word rhythms. *[More than one volunteer? Take turns or create a bass section.]* We're not going to play the bass just yet, but get ready. And when we start—remember to tap, not pound, the beat.

3 Okay. Next we're going to choose one word from each column, starting with column 4 and going down to column 1. *[Print the selected 4 words on the board in order from 4-syllable to 1-syllable.]*

4 Now we're going to say the words and tap out their rhythm on our desks, like this: *alligator, hummingbird, donkey, fish. [Tap once for each syllable, in a regular rhythm— there will be a quiet beat between your 3-syllable and 2-syllable words and a quiet beat after your 1-syllable word.]* Let's try that together. *[Practice it.]* Great. Now let's tap them out three times. Then we'll select four different words to play.

FOLLOW-UP

Invite students to introduce themselves. As each student says his or her name, have the class "play" the name on their desktops.

VARIATION

Do an Internet search for "Teaching with Music" to find more ideas. A number of good resources offer free lesson plans.

Taken from *Kick-Start Your Class: Academic Icebreakers to Engage Students.* Copyright © 2012 by LouAnne Johnson. Reproduced by permission of Jossey-Bass, an Imprint of Wiley. www.josseybass.com.

65. WHAT'S MY NUMBER?

☆ **PURPOSE**: math icebreaker: getting acquainted   ☆ **AGES**: 6–adult

☆ **TIME**: 10–20 minutes

☆ **MATERIALS**: index cards and markers

PREPARATION

Create a simple poster showing five different numbers, written large enough to be seen easily from anywhere in the room. Or write the five numbers on the board. Each number should represent something from your life. For example: 2 dogs, 3 children, 4 bowling trophies, 6 autographed baseballs, 207 music CDs, and so on. Include at least one number for something intangible, such as 20 for the number of times each day you try to remember to be grateful for the good things in your life.

INSTRUCTIONS FOR STUDENTS

1 On the board (or poster) you will see five numbers. Each of those numbers represents something from my life. Your job is to guess what those numbers represent. This is not a graded activity, so don't worry about getting it right.

2 What do you think this first number represents? *[If nobody answers or raises a hand, select a student who is making eye contact and ask him or her to make a guess. Go through each of your numbers.]*

3 Now I'm going to distribute index cards and markers for you to write down your own number. Just one number, please. And it doesn't have to be personal. You could choose number 2 to represent how many shoes you are wearing.

4 You will have one minute to write down your number. Then we'll go around the room. When it's your turn, hold up your card so everybody can see your number. Then we will all try to guess what your number represents.

FOLLOW-UP

Repeat this activity as a class or in small groups as a way to continue getting acquainted and building connections between people.

VARIATION

Divide students into small groups and let them play the game privately. This works for very large classes when you don't have a lot of time, and for classes where you have shy students or those who are not comfortable being in the spotlight. (English language learners, for example, may hesitate to speak in public until they begin gaining confidence over time.)

WHAT'S MY NUMBER?

106

Chapter Seven

Scientific Suggestions

Science is a natural subject for icebreakers and group activities because the elements of discovery and surprise are key to the study of science—and human brains are wired to seek novelty. This seeking is not a result of boredom, but rather a survival mechanism.

Our left-brain hemispheres remain on constant alert for incoming stimuli from the environment. When teachers provide new and different activities and experiences, they engage student brains and prime them for learning new information and skills.

Among the activities in this chapter is Tower Builders from the Public Broadcasting Service website for children: visit *www.pbskids.org/zoom*. This website offers dozens of lessons and activities, many suggested or designed by students themselves. It's an excellent resource for teachers and is among those included in the Appendix of this book.

66. CRITTER CONNECTION

☆ **PURPOSE:** science icebreaker   ☆ **AGES:** 7–18

☆ **TIME:** 10–15 minutes

☆ **MATERIALS:** picture, name, or description cards; poster board or paper and markers

PREPARATION

Create photo or illustration cards featuring a collection of living creatures (farm animals, wild animals, mammals, arachnids, insects, amphibians, and so on). For young learners, use familiar creatures. To make the assignment more challenging for older students, use different classes or species and/or skip the picture cards.

Print the name of each critter on a separate card. Print a description of each critter on a separate card.

Greet students as they enter the classroom, handing each student an illustration, name card, or description card.

Before you begin the activity, demonstrate your Attention Getter (see the Introduction for details).

INSTRUCTIONS FOR STUDENTS

1 Each person has a picture card, a name card, or a description of a particular insect (mammal, invertebrate, and so on).

2 When I give the signal to begin, you will have ___ minutes to locate the people whose cards correspond to yours.

3 Once you locate your group, your task is to create a poster about your critter, giving as much information as you can.

FOLLOW-UP

Ask each group to present its critter to the class. Give groups the option of appointing a spokesperson or presenting as a team if they need the moral support.

If time permits, assign students the task of researching their critters to find additional information, such as location found, life span, mating habits, and so on.

(continued)

(continued)

VARIATIONS

Create enough picture cards so that each student will have his or her own picture. Assign them the task of creating the name and description cards using materials in the classroom or in the library. Share when they are all finished.

For nonreaders or non-English speakers, create two or more copies of the same critter picture and have students find the partner who has the matching picture. The teacher then provides the name of the critter, and students share what they know about each critter. As a follow-up, let them research their critters.

Create matching pairs of picture cards. Divide students into teams and let them play Critter Concentration, where they turn all the cards face down and take turns selecting two cards, trying to match the pairs. *(See Team Classroom Concentration in Chapter Five for instructions on playing the concentration game.)*

67. IT'S ELEMENTAL

☆ **PURPOSE:** science icebreaker   ☆ **AGES:** 7–adult
☆ **TIME:** 10–20 minutes
☆ **MATERIALS:** cards containing chemical element names and symbols

PREPARATION

Divide the number of students on your roster by two. Create pairs of cards, one with the name and one with the symbol for each element (for example, barium and Ba, silver and Ag). Create enough pairs for each student to receive one card. (Make 2–3 extra pairs for students who may be added to your roster at the last minute.)

Shuffle the cards so they are in random order. As students enter your classroom, greet them and give each person a card.

INSTRUCTIONS FOR STUDENTS

1 Each person has a card that shows either the name of a chemical element or the symbol for that element. When I give the signal to begin, your job is to find the person whose card corresponds to yours.

2 You will have __ minutes to find your partner. This will be the signal that your time is up. [Demonstrate your Attention Getter—see the Introduction for details.]

3 After you have found your partners, your next task is to use your textbook, the computer, or reference books in the library to create a drawing that shows the atomic structure of your element. Here is a sample. [Show them a sample drawing.]

(continued)

(continued)

FOLLOW-UP

Invite students to share their drawings. Post them on the wall to create your own chart. (For a complete chart, you will have to repeat the activity.)

If time permits, let students create sets of element cards (names and symbols) and use them to play Elemental Concentration, where they turn all the cards facedown and take turns selecting two cards, trying to match cards. As each match is located, students remove it from the table until all the cards have been matched.

VARIATIONS

For younger students, use the most familiar elements, such as calcium, barium, and radium. Increase the challenge for older students by using less familiar elements, such as lanthanum, cerium, and berkelium.

If you have Internet access in your classroom or library, allow students to visit the website *www.chemicalelements.com*, where they will find an interactive periodic table of elements. They can click on a symbol for more information about each element, such as atomic structure, number, and mass; melting and boiling points; and density and color.

68. IS THAT A FACT?

☆ **PURPOSE**: science icebreaker　　☆ **AGES**: 7–adult

☆ **TIME**: 5–15 minutes

☆ **MATERIALS**: poster board or slides and projector, 5 × 7 index cards and markers

PREPARATION

Create posters or slides containing correct and incorrect scientific statements. For example:

Simple. Spiders are insects.

Intermediate. The sun is 93,000,000 miles away from Earth.

Challenging. Lemons are acidic, but when they are eaten they have an alkalizing effect on the human body.

Give each student two index cards and a bold marker.

INSTRUCTIONS FOR STUDENTS

1 Today we're going to look at some scientific facts and fallacies. This activity is not graded. It's a science warm-up for your brain.

2 Your first task is to write *Yes* on one of your cards and *No* on the other one. Please write in large letters, so that I can see them from a distance. You have __ seconds to make your cards. Go. *[Pause while students create cards.]*

3 I am going to display a poster (or slide) that contains a statement. Your job is to decide whether the statement is a fact or if it's incorrect. If you believe the statement is a fact, hold up your Yes card. If you think it's false, hold up No.

4 You will have __ seconds to respond to each statement. This will be the signal that your time is up. *[Demonstrate your Attention Getter—see the Introduction for details.]*

After each statement, pause to count the number of correct answers. Choose a student who has the correct answer to explain why the statement is or is not a fact.

FOLLOW-UP

Be sure to allow enough time for students to actually think about the statements instead of feeling rushed to respond. Some highly intelligent students are slow processors who need time to think. Also, if you have English language learners, they may be mentally translating back and forth from their native languages, which takes a bit of time.

Assign students to work in pairs or teams. Give them 15 minutes to come up with 5–10 facts or fallacies of their own that pertain to information they have recently learned. Repeat this activity periodically, using the students' statements.

VARIATION

If you have individual whiteboards available, give each student a dry-erase marker and an eraser or paper towel. Have them write *Yes* or *No* in response to each statement.

IS THAT A FACT?

Taken from *Kick-Start Your Class: Academic Icebreakers to Engage Students.* Copyright © 2012 by LouAnne Johnson.
Reproduced by permission of Jossey-Bass, an Imprint of Wiley. www.josseybass.com.

69. MAIL CALL

⭐ **PURPOSE**: science icebreaker   ⭐ **AGES**: 7–adult

⭐ **TIME**: 10–30 minutes

⭐ **MATERIALS**: typed letters that ask science-related questions

PREPARATION

Create a series of age-appropriate letters that pose questions about science-related topics. For example:

→ What's the difference between an alligator and a crocodile?

→ What four-legged animal can run the fastest? How fast can it run?

→ My kitchen sink is clogged. My sister told me that I could dump a cup of vinegar into the drain, then add a cup of baking soda and pour a cup of boiling water on it. What would happen if I did that? Would it clear my drain? Is it safe?

Before beginning the activity, assign students to work in pairs or teams (see Chapter Three for quick and easy ways to assign work teams).

INSTRUCTIONS FOR STUDENTS

1 I'm going to give each pair (or team) a letter that asks a question. Your job is to write an answer.

2 This is not a graded activity. You earn full credit for participating, whether your answer is right or wrong. Don't worry about making a mistake. Some of the most important scientific discoveries were the result of mistakes. *[Give age-appropriate examples of mistakes.]*

3 You will have __ minutes to discuss your letter and prepare your answer.

4 This will be the signal that your time is up. *[Demonstrate your Attention Getter—see the Introduction for details.]*

FOLLOW-UP

Discuss each question and answer as a class.

Assign students to work in pairs or teams. Have each team write a letter that asks a science-related question, then collect the letters and distribute them to teams. (You could add the requirement that letters pertain to a recently studied unit.) Give students 5–10 minutes to prepare a written or oral response. Invite students to share their letters and responses.

VARIATIONS

Allow students to present their responses orally, instead of writing them. If computers are available, have students type their responses and/or letters. You might also allow them to use the Internet to research their questions.

Taken from *Kick-Start Your Class: Academic Icebreakers to Engage Students.* Copyright © 2012 by LouAnne Johnson. Reproduced by permission of Jossey-Bass, an Imprint of Wiley. www.josseybass.com.

70. RECYCLED ANIMALS

☆ **PURPOSE:** science icebreaker   ☆ **AGES:** 7-16

☆ **TIME:** 10-20 minutes

☆ **MATERIALS:** assorted odds and ends (see Preparation section), scissors, wire, tape

PREPARATION

Assemble a large collection of odd objects such as empty toilet paper rolls, matchsticks, wire hangers or paper clips, biodegradable packing puffs, bubble wrap, and buttons.

Before you begin the activity, assign students to work in pairs *(see Chapter Three for some quick and easy methods of assigning work partners).*

INSTRUCTIONS FOR STUDENTS

1. Your mission is to create a unique animal using any of the materials provided. Your animal can be real or imaginary. The only requirement is that it must have at least one moving part.

2. You will have __ minutes to create your animal. This will be your signal that time is up. *[Demonstrate your Attention Getter signal—see the Introduction for details.]*

3. When we finish, we will share and discuss our menagerie.

FOLLOW-UP

Ask students to take turns sharing their animal inventions. Or leave the inventions on their desks and have students circulate the room and view each one, trying to guess its identity.

VARIATION

Increase the challenge by requiring animals with four legs and a tail or some other appendage or attribute.

71. TOWER BUILDERS

☆ **PURPOSE**: science icebreaker   ☆ **AGES**: 7–adult

☆ **TIME**: 10–20 minutes

☆ **MATERIALS**: newspapers and tape

PREPARATION

Assemble enough newspapers to give two full sheets to each pair or team of students in your class. Place the newspapers where students have easy access to them.

Before beginning the activity, assign students to work in pairs or teams (see Chapter Three for quick and easy ways to randomly assign work teams). Demonstrate your Attention Getter before you begin.

INSTRUCTIONS FOR STUDENTS

1 Before we begin our tower-building activity, I want to ask you to consider this question: Do you think you will be able to build the tallest tower by using paper only or by using paper and tape together? [Discuss student answers.]

2 Now it's time to test our theories. Your first mission is to build the tallest possible tower using only two sheets of newspaper. When I say "Go," you will have __ minutes to get two sheets of paper and build your tower.

3 This will be your signal that the time is up. [Demonstrate your Attention Getter—see the Introduction for details.]

FOLLOW-UP

Measure the paper-only towers and have students record their results on paper or on the board.

Repeat the activity, but this time let students use two sheets of paper and tape. Distribute individual tape dispensers to each pair or team. Build the paper-tape towers and compare the results to the paper-only towers. (In most cases, the paper-only tower will be taller because the tape will create imbalance.)

Ask students to share their experiences and conclusions about using paper or paper plus tape to build the paper towers.

Ask students to write a brief summary of their tower-building experience and what they learned from the activity.

VARIATION

Visit the website *www.pbskids.org/zoom*. Select "Activities from the Show," then choose an activity that is age-appropriate for your class. Or allow students to browse the site and select their own activities.

TOWER BUILDERS

72. WHAT IS THIS?

☆ **PURPOSE:** science icebreaker   ☆ **AGES:** 7-adult

☆ **TIME:** 10-20 minutes

☆ **MATERIALS:** photos or portions of photos from magazines

PREPARATION

Using a digital camera, or by cutting and enlarging pieces of pictures from magazines, create a series of visuals that show extreme close-ups of various plants and animals: for example, the tip of a zebra's tail, one arm of an octopus, and a single rose petal.

The older your students, the more challenging the visuals should be. Make enough for each student to have two, or each pair or team to have three to four different visuals.

Create a numbered template for each student (or pair or team) to write down the names of the plants or animals in their pictures.

Before beginning the activity, assign students to work in pairs or teams (see Chapter Three for quick and easy methods of randomly assigning work partners). Also, demonstrate your Attention Getter, which will signal that time is up (see the Introduction for details).

INSTRUCTIONS FOR STUDENTS

1. Each person (or pair or team) has some pictures of familiar plants and animals—but the pictures show only a small portion of those plants or animals. Your job is to identify what is shown in your pictures.

2. You will have __ minutes to write down the names of the plants or animals in your pictures. This will be the signal that time is up. *[Demonstrate your Attention Getter.]*

3. We'll go around the room, take a look at each other's pictures, and see how many we correctly identified.

4. Then we'll tack all the pictures to the bulletin board so we can all see them.

FOLLOW-UP

If time permits, instead of looking at all the pictures at once, have students pass their visuals to the next student or team and repeat the activity one or more times.

VARIATION

Instead of creating physical visuals, create a slide show. Ask students to work quietly together to identify each slide as you show it. Provide a numbered template for them to write the name of the plant or animal shown on each slide. After you have viewed all the slides, check to see which pair or team correctly identified the most visuals.

Chapter Eight

Language Arts Starters

*B*ecause language arts is required curriculum for virtually every grade level in every school, this chapter includes a larger selection of icebreakers than some of the others.

But these activities can be used effectively in other classes to enhance and support cross-curriculum skill development. And most of the activities can be tweaked and adapted to suit a wide variety of student ages, abilities, and personalities. Wacky Wordies, for example, are popular with everybody from elementary students to retirees, because they make thinking genuinely fun.

73. ANALOGY ANCHORS

☆ **PURPOSE:** language arts icebreaker   ☆ **AGES:** 10–adult

☆ **TIME:** 10–20 minutes

☆ **MATERIALS:** index cards

PREPARATION

Create a list of analogies that will be challenging but not too difficult for your students to understand. An online search will provide many samples, such as these:

Simple

   finger : hand :: toe : foot

Intermediate

   bait : fish :: nectar : bee

Advanced

   abstract : Pollock :: impressionist : Monet

Divide the number of students on your roster by two to find the number of analogies you will need. Make a couple of extras to have on hand in case of unexpected arrivals. If you end up with an uneven number of students, either give one student two anchor cards or participate in the activity yourself. Do not leave anybody out.

Create two index cards for each analogy, with half on each card. "Finger : hand" would be on one card and "toe : foot" on the other. Mark the back of the first card from each pair with an X to indicate your analogy anchors.

Copy one or two sample analogies on the board (*not* those on the cards).

Greet students at the door and give each student one card. Ask them to be seated and await instructions.

INSTRUCTIONS FOR STUDENTS

1 Everybody has a card containing one half of an analogy. Who can explain what an analogy is? [*Discuss. If students are hesitant to speak, explain it and move on.*]

2 Let's look at the samples on the board. Can somebody explain the first one? [*Discuss.*]

3 Please look on the back of your card now. If your card has an X, you are an anchor. You have 60 seconds to come up and form a line facing the class. Go! [*Pause.*] Excellent. Since you are anchors, you will not move during this activity.

(continued)

ANALOGY ANCHORS

Taken from *Kick-Start Your Class: Academic Icebreakers to Engage Students.* Copyright © 2012 by LouAnne Johnson. Reproduced by permission of Jossey-Bass, an Imprint of Wiley. www.josseybass.com.

(continued)

4. People whose cards don't have Xs now have ___ minutes to find their anchors to complete their analogies. Please help each other so we can meet our deadline. Ready? Go!

FOLLOW-UP

Ask each analogy pair to hold up their cards and read them. Ask a volunteer to explain the relationship between each analogy pair. Discuss as a class.

Collect all the cards and ask for two volunteers to see if they can match them all up correctly, with or without the help of classmates.

74. A PICTURE TELLS A HUNDRED WORDS

☆ **PURPOSE:** language arts icebreaker   ☆ **AGES:** 7–adult

☆ **TIME:** 10–20 minutes

☆ **MATERIALS:** selection of pictures, drawings, or paintings

PREPARATION

Find or create age-appropriate artworks that present thought-provoking subjects, scenes, or designs. Create a large poster that can be displayed or a slide for each illustration that can be projected. If you can't enlarge the art to create posters or if you don't have a computer or projector to display the slides, then create individual handouts for students. You may opt to give each student a different piece of art or make copies of the same art for the entire class.

INSTRUCTIONS FOR STUDENTS

1. You have probably heard the saying, "A picture is worth a thousand words." What does that saying mean to you? *[Discuss student responses. If nobody responds, share your own ideas and move ahead.]*

2. Today our challenge is to come up with 100 words to describe a picture.

3. First, we'll all take a look at a picture and take a minute to think about it. Then we're all going to write down on our papers the first 100 words that come to our minds when we look at the picture.

4. This isn't a test, and there are no right or wrong answers. We're just going to stretch our brains and our vocabularies a bit to warm them up. You can just write down words or you can write full sentences—it's up to you.

5. We're going to take __ minutes to write our words. This will be the signal that time is up. *[Demonstrate your Attention Getter—see the Introduction for details.]*

FOLLOW-UP

Go around the room and ask students to share one word from their lists. Ask for a volunteer to write the words on the board. Ask for another volunteer to count the words and let you know when you have reached 100. Discuss the words the students have suggested.

VARIATION

Instead of asking students to write down their words on paper, invite them to come to the board and write their words. Ask for a volunteer to tally the word count. Challenge students to continue for another 50 or 100 words if they seem engaged and motivated.

75. CANINE CONNECTION

☆ **PURPOSE**: language arts icebreaker
☆ **AGES**: 7–adult
☆ **TIME**: 10–20 minutes
☆ **MATERIALS**: pictures of adult dogs and puppies

PREPARATION

Divide the number of students on your roster by three to find the number of different dog breeds you will need for this activity.

Assemble a collection of pictures (or draw your own) featuring adult dogs of various different breeds. For each adult dog, include two identical puppy pictures of the same breed. (Make a few extra puppy cards for unexpected arrivals. Or participate yourself to even the numbers so no students are left out.)

On the board, print the following two quotations in large letters:

You can't teach an old dog new tricks.

You can't run with the big dogs if you pee like a puppy.

Greet students at the door as they arrive and hand each one a dog or puppy picture. Ask them to be seated and wait for instructions.

INSTRUCTIONS FOR STUDENTS

1. Everybody has a picture of a dog or a puppy from one of several breeds. There is one adult dog picture and two (or three) puppies from each breed.

2. When I say "Go," you will have ___ minutes to find the people who have the same breed of dog as yours. You can ask each other for help, but you cannot exchange pictures.

3. Here is the signal that will let you know your time is up. *[Demonstrate your Attention Getter—see the Introduction for details.]*

4. When you hear the signal, it's time for your group to begin the next task. You will have ___ minutes to discuss the two quotations on the board with your group and figure out how they relate to us as students or as people. There is no right or wrong answer. This is a thinking activity. Everybody earns full credit for participating.

5. Ready? Begin.

FOLLOW-UP

Invite each group to share their response to the quotations. Give each group a round of applause after they finish.

VARIATIONS

For younger students, skip the quotations or use only one of the quotations. Or use a variety of different animals such as big pig—little pig and big duck—little duck. To assign pairs instead of groups, make only one puppy picture for each breed.

CANINE CONNECTION

76. CONTRACTION CUTTERS

☆ **PURPOSE:** language arts icebreaker   ☆ **AGES:** 6-9

☆ **TIME:** 10-20 minutes

☆ **MATERIALS:** butcher paper, 8.5 × 11 paper, scissors, markers, glue sticks

PREPARATION

Create a chart showing 5-10 familiar contractions (such as *can't*, *don't*, and *it's*) on a large piece of butcher paper in letters large enough to be seen from a distance. On a piece of 8.5 × 11 paper, print all the words from which the contractions in your lesson are made (such as *cannot*, *do not*, and *it is*). Make copies of the word list to distribute to students.

Choose one of the contractions to use as a model for students. Print the contraction in large letters on a sheet of paper. Print the corresponding full words on another sheet of paper. Before students begin the exercise, model it for them—cut up the full word, remove the appropriate letters, and paste the letters on a blank sheet to form the contraction. Add an apostrophe with your marker.

After you model the activity, give each student a copy of the full word list and a blank sheet of paper. Provide scissors and tape or glue.

INSTRUCTIONS FOR STUDENTS

1. Your mission is to create contractions using the words on your list. If your brain needs a little boost, you can look at my chart to guide you.

2. First, cut out each word. Cut out the letters that won't be in the contraction.

3. Next glue your letters onto the blank page to create the contraction—don't forget to leave space for the apostrophe.

4. Use your marker to add an apostrophe in the correct place.

5. We'll work on these for ___ minutes and see where we are. Here is the signal you will hear when those minutes have passed. *[Demonstrate your Attention Getter.]*

FOLLOW-UP

Ask for volunteers to stand up and show their contraction list. Or ask students to come to your desk one at a time and show you their lists. Ask them to read the contractions out loud and tell you what they mean.

VARIATION

To aid students who are visual learners, consider printing each contraction in a different color marker and copy the words to be cut on pastel paper that matches the word color. For example, print *can't* in blue letters on the poster and make copies of the word *cannot* on blue paper.

(continued)

CONTRACTION CUTTERS

Taken from *Kick-Start Your Class: Academic Icebreakers to Engage Students.* Copyright © 2012 by LouAnne Johnson. Reproduced by permission of Jossey-Bass, an Imprint of Wiley. www.josseybass.com.

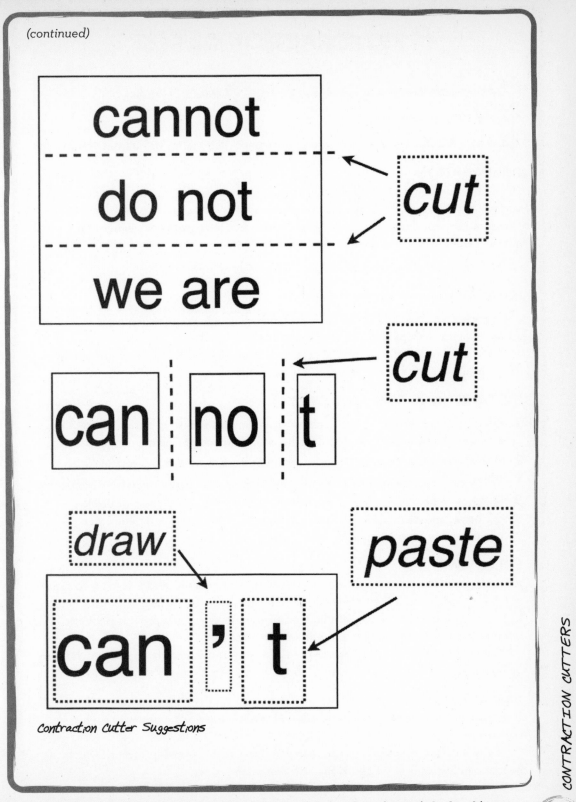

Contraction Cutter Suggestions

77. FOREIGN PHRASES

☆ **PURPOSE**: language arts icebreaker   ☆ **AGES**: 9–adult

☆ **TIME**: 10–20 minutes

☆ **MATERIALS**: index cards, foreign language dictionaries or Internet connection

PREPARATION

Divide the number of students on your roster by two to get the number of phrases you will need. Search the Internet or use textbooks and foreign language dictionaries to assemble a list of foreign phrases. If possible, choose proverbs or sayings that offer advice. Here are two good sources to start with:

http://www.omniglot.com/language/phrases/index.htm

http://users.elite.net/runner/jennifers

Copy each phrase and the name of its language (such as Greek, Chinese, or Arabic) on an index card. Copy the translation on a separate card.

Greet students as they enter the classroom and hand each person one of the index cards. Ask them to be seated and wait for instructions.

INSTRUCTIONS FOR STUDENTS

1 Everybody has an index card that contains a foreign phrase or a translation of a phrase in English. Your job is to find the person whose phrase matches yours.

2 When I say, "Begin," you will have __ minutes to match your phrase or translation. When you hear this signal, it means the time is up. *[Demonstrate your Attention Getter.]*

3 Feel free to help each other if you recognize any words. And you may use the textbooks and dictionaries in the room, as well as the Internet *(or any other resources you have on hand)*. Ready? Begin.

FOLLOW-UP

Ask each pair to share their phrase and translation. Encourage students to try to sound out the phrases, even if they aren't correct. This helps them realize how difficult it can be to learn a foreign language with no context to help. If you can provide phonetic pronunciations for the phrases, share them with students.

Collect the cards and redistribute them. See how quickly students can match them up now that they have heard the translations. Encourage them to help each other.

VARIATIONS

To form 3-student teams, include 2 cards with each phrase or 2 cards with each translation.

If you have many Spanish speakers in your classes, use popular *"dichos,"* which can be found online or in any English-Spanish dictionary.

78. "I AM" POEMS

☆ **PURPOSE:** reading icebreakers   ☆ **AGES:** 6–adult

☆ **TIME:** 10–20 minutes

☆ **MATERIALS:** "I Am" templates, markers (optional)

PREPARATION

Create a template for students to fill in, with the following starters:

I am _____

I like _____

I don't like _____

Some day, I would like to _____

Greet students at the door as they enter the classroom. Hand each student a copy of the template and ask them to be seated.

INSTRUCTIONS FOR STUDENTS

1. Today we're going to introduce ourselves. But you don't have to stand in front of the class to introduce yourself—we're going to let our poetry speak for us.

2. On your template, you have four sentences that aren't finished. After you fill in the blanks, you will have written your "I Am" poem.

3. You will have __ minutes to finish your poems.

4. When you are finished, please raise your hand and I will come and collect your poem.

5. After I have collected all the poems, I will read them out loud one at a time. After I read your poem, I will ask you to take your poem and tack it to the bulletin board.

6. Once all the poems are posted, we will have a word picture of us as a class.

FOLLOW-UP

After you read each poem, ask its author to stand and identify him- or herself.

VARIATIONS

If students appear to be comfortable, invite each student to stand and read his or her own poem instead of having the teacher read them. Give each student a round of applause or a class thumbs-up.

If time permits, provide markers and let students illustrate their poems.

79. MEANINGFUL MATCHES

☆ **PURPOSE:** language arts icebreaker

☆ **TIME:** 10-20 minutes

☆ **MATERIALS:** index cards, dictionary, Internet (optional)

☆ **AGES:** 8-adult

*Vocab.
Game
for freshmen
& seniors*

PREPARATION

Divide the number of students on your roster by two to find the number of vocabulary words you will need for this activity. Create a couple of extra word or definition cards and set them aside for use in case additional students arrive unexpectedly.

Print each vocabulary word in large letters on an index card. Print the definition for each word on a separate card.

Greet students as they enter the room and give each one an index card. Invite them to be seated and wait for instructions.

INSTRUCTIONS FOR STUDENTS

1. Everybody has an index card. Half of the index cards have vocabulary words printed on them. The other half of the cards have definitions.

2. Your job is to find the person who has the word or definition that matches your card.

3. You will have __ minutes to match your cards correctly. This will be your signal that time is up. *[Demonstrate your Attention Getter—see the Introduction for details.]*

4. Feel free to help each other if you know the definition of a word. And you may use the dictionary or the computer *(if you have one in your classroom)* to look up the definitions.

5. Ready? Begin.

FOLLOW-UP

Ask students to draw illustrations for their vocabulary words. Or ask them to act out the words.

VARIATIONS

Ask students to find challenging words in the dictionary and create their own vocabulary word or definition cards. Collect all the cards, distribute them, and see how long it takes to match them up correctly. Do this activity using roots and prefixes instead of words and definitions.

80. LICK A SLUG

☆ **PURPOSE**: language arts icebreaker   ☆ **AGES**: 7–adult

☆ **TIME**: 10–20 minutes

☆ **MATERIALS**: age-appropriate "wise" quotations

PREPARATION

If possible, read the book *When You Lick a Slug, Your Tongue Goes Numb*, by H. Jackson Brown Jr. (Rutledge Hill Press, 1995), which is a collection of wise sayings from elementary and secondary school students. Here are a few samples:

"If you put a frog in a girl's shirt, get ready for some screaming."

"Never sneeze when you are chewing a mouthful of nuts."

"When teachers get old, like over 50, they get real crabby."

If you can't find a copy of the book, print a copy of the cover from an online bookseller. Then create your own wise sayings and illustrations or locate some other source.

Post several different illustrated sayings on the walls or bulletin board of your classroom.

Greet students as they enter the room and invite them to browse and discuss the sayings that are posted.

INSTRUCTIONS FOR STUDENTS

1. Our writing activity today was inspired by the book *When You Lick a Slug, Your Tongue Goes Numb. [If you have a copy of the cover, show it to students.]* The book is a collection of wise sayings by students.

2. Today we're going to write and illustrate our own wise sayings. What advice would you give to little kids who are just starting school? Or what important thing have you learned about getting along in school?

3. If you are a good artist, please raise your hand. *[Pause.]* These are the people you can ask if you need some help with your illustration. But please don't worry about being perfect. Everybody is an artist. And this isn't a contest—it's meant to be fun.

FOLLOW-UP

If students feel comfortable, invite them to share their sayings with the class. For groups with shy students, give them the choice of posting their saying on the board without presenting it to the class. After all of the sayings are posted, invite students to browse and admire them.

VARIATION

Instead of posting sayings on the wall or bulletin board, create a slide show and project them on a screen for students to view one at a time before you ask them to write their own sayings.

81. MIRROR WRITING

group activity

☆ **PURPOSE**: language arts icebreaker   ☆ **AGES**: 8–adult

☆ **TIME**: 10–20 minutes

☆ **MATERIALS**: whiteboard or screen, paper and pencils or pens

PREPARATION

Print a provocative question or comment on the board or project it on a screen.

Greet students as they enter the room and invite them to take a seat. Ask them to read the question or comment and think about it silently until everybody is seated.

Before you begin the activity, assign students to work in pairs. (See Chapter Three for quick and easy methods of randomly assigning partners.) Ask partners to sit facing each other for the activity.

Distribute paper and pens or pencils.

INSTRUCTIONS FOR STUDENTS

1. We're going to do a writing exercise called Mirror Writing. The idea is that everybody will write down their response to the question or comment on the board. Then you'll exchange papers with your partners and discuss your responses.

2. It's fine to ask questions or disagree with each other, but keep it friendly and respectful. Different viewpoints make the world a more interesting place. Imagine how boring it would be if everybody thought the same thoughts and liked the same things.

3. You will have __ minutes to write your response. This will be your signal that time is up. [*Demonstrate your Attention Getter—see the Introduction for details.*]

4. Then you will have __ minutes to discuss your responses.

5. Don't worry about spelling and grammar or writing perfect sentences. Right now we're focusing on sharing our ideas. Ready? Let's begin.

FOLLOW-UP

If students are engaged and motivated, try the exercise again with a different prompt. Or ask students to suggest prompts. (If you receive multiple suggestions, repeat the activity later occasionally, using student prompts.)

VARIATION

Repeat the activity, but have students sit back-to-back and exchange their papers without turning around, so they read them without facing each other and without discussing them. Ask for feedback, comparing the two different experiences. *Did they prefer discussing their writing, or did they prefer to let it speak for itself?*

82. MUSICAL WORDS

af Vocabulary

☆ **PURPOSE:** language arts icebreaker
☆ **AGES:** 6–adult
☆ **TIME:** 10–20 minutes
☆ **MATERIALS:** short musical excerpts, paper and pencils

PREPARATION

Prepare several short excerpts of a variety of instrumental music, including classical, pop, big band, blues, folk, jazz, and popular local music, if possible.

Provide each student with paper and pencil.

Before you begin the activity, demonstrate your Attention Getter, which will indicate time is up or that you need everybody's quiet attention.

INSTRUCTIONS FOR STUDENTS

1. We're going to do an exercise called Musical Words. I'm going to play a selection of different songs, all instrumental, with no lyrics or singing. Your job is to write down whatever words come to mind when you hear each song.

2. We'll start with 10 words for the first song. Then we'll try 20 words for the second song and so on. And we'll see if we can think of 50 words for the fifth song. This isn't a test, and everybody earns full credit for participating.

3. The first song will last 30 seconds. And each song after that will last a little bit longer, since we will be writing more words for each new song.

4. Would anybody like to volunteer to be the timer? You can be the timer and participate in writing the words, or you can simply be the timer. It's your choice. *[If you have multiple volunteers, let them take turns, one per song.]*

FOLLOW-UP

After each song, ask for volunteers to share their word lists and explain their choices. If students are motivated to continue the discussion, play it by ear, depending on the amount of time you have to devote to this activity.

VARIATIONS

To increase the challenge, ask students to write only adjectives when they listen to the first song, nouns when they listen to the second, colors when they listen to the third, and so on.

For very young students, skip the word lists and ask them to say their words as the music is softly playing. Write their words on the board as they say them.

83. PICTOGRAPHS

"The Miracle Worker"

☆ **PURPOSE**: language arts icebreaker   ☆ **AGES**: 7–adult

☆ **TIME**: 10–30 minutes

☆ **MATERIALS**: paper, pencils, pens, markers

PREPARATION

Find or create some pictographs that are age-appropriate for your class. An online search will give you many examples such as "No Smoking" or "Poison." Here are a couple of resources for interesting pictographs:

> *http://jordankb24.blogspot.com/2010_09_01_archive.html* (forest service symbols)

> *http://www.inquiry.net/images/uisl076.gif* (Sioux and Ojibwa symbols)

Make individual copies of the pictogram(s) for students, or project them on a screen that is visible to everybody.

INSTRUCTIONS FOR STUDENTS

1. Let's think of all the ways people communicate without talking. *[Possible responses include writing, body language, gestures, drawing, and other arts.]*

2. Today we're going to communicate our ideas through pictures. Here are some samples of pictographs—pictures that express an idea, tell a story, or give information or a warning. *[Distribute samples or project them on the screen.]*

3. Your mission today is to create one pictograph. Your pictograph can be about anything you choose. You could draw two people shaking hands to show they are friends. Or you could make a sign to show that there is a skateboard park.

4. Don't worry—this isn't a contest, and your art doesn't have to be professional. Everybody earns full credit for participating.

5. If you need help, raise your hand and I will discuss your ideas with you. And if you are a good artist, feel free to help your classmates with their art.

6. We'll work on our pictographs for 10 minutes and then I will give you this signal. *[Demonstrate your Attention Getter—see the Introduction for details.]* At that time, we'll see what we have. If you don't have time to finish, don't worry. You can work on this again later. Or you can take it home and work on it and bring it back tomorrow.

(continued)

(continued)

FOLLOW-UP

Post the pictographs on the bulletin board. Let students browse and discuss them.

Teach a lesson about interpreting and creating pictographs. There are many samples online, including this one: *http://www.mathisfun.com/data/pictographs.html*

VARIATION

Provide 3 or 4 sample topics for students to illustrate, such as various emotions (anger, fear, and surprise) or verbs (skiing, skating, and swimming).

84. POETRY-PICTURE MATCH

☆ **PURPOSE**: language arts icebreaker   ☆ **AGES**: 6–adult

☆ **TIME**: 10–20 minutes

☆ **MATERIALS**: selection of photos or illustrations, 3–4 poems

PREPARATION

Assemble a large selection of photos, drawings, and illustrations of various people, landscapes, animals, abstract and impressionist art, and familiar and unfamiliar objects.

Select 3–4 age-appropriate poems that vividly evoke a mood or emotion. Make enough copies of the poems to give each student a copy.

Greet students at the door as they enter the classroom. Give each student a copy of the poems. Ask them to take a seat and quickly scan the poems.

INSTRUCTIONS FOR STUDENTS

1 We all know that good poetry depends on good word choices. But today we're going to consider how our eyes and hearts respond to poetry, in addition to how it sounds to our ears.

2 I'm going to ask for a volunteer to read each poem aloud. Don't worry. If you're feeling shy today, I will read them. I love poetry, and it's meant to be read aloud so we can hear how carefully the poet selected just the right words.

3 After we read each poem, I'm going to ask you to choose a picture or illustration that you think "matches" the poem in some way. You will have __ minutes to select your picture and return to your seat.

4 You will hear this signal when the time is up. *[Demonstrate your Attention Getter— see the Introduction for details.]* Okay. Let's begin.

FOLLOW-UP

Ask for volunteers to display the art they selected and explain why.

VARIATIONS

Instead of reading each poem aloud, assign students to work in pairs and read the poems aloud to each other. Then they select the art. When they are finished, the teacher discusses their art choices with them.

Instead of distributing paper copies of the poems, project them on a screen and ask students to select the art that complements the poetry.

Provide markers or paint and ask students to create their own art for each poem.

85. PROOFREADING PAIRS

☆ **PURPOSE:** language arts icebreaker   ☆ **AGES:** 7–adult

☆ **TIME:** 10–20 minutes

☆ **MATERIALS:** letter or article that contains spelling or grammar mistakes

PREPARATION

Prepare an age-appropriate letter or magazine-style article that contains a number of grammar and spelling errors. Make a list of the errors for your own reference. Make enough copies of the letter or article so you have enough for each student.

Greet students as they enter your classroom. Hand each one a copy of the letter or article. Ask them to find a seat and take a quick look at the letter or article and wait for instructions.

Before you begin the activity, assign students to work in pairs. (See Chapter Three for quick and easy methods of random assignment that don't leave anybody out.)

INSTRUCTIONS FOR STUDENTS

1. If you look closely, you will see that the letter or article I gave you has some spelling and grammar errors. There are __ errors.

2. Your job is to work with your partner to see if you can find and correct all of the errors.

3. When you have found all __ errors, please raise your hand. I will come to your desk and see the corrections you have made.

FOLLOW-UP

As a class, ask for a volunteer to explain why each correction was necessary. Give each person who volunteers a quick round of applause or a whole-class thumbs-up.

As a follow-up, ask students to create their own articles or letters containing errors. After they finish, they exchange papers with another pair and see if they can find all the necessary corrections.

VARIATION

To increase the challenge, don't tell students how many errors they should find. Let them do the activity and then decide among themselves how many corrections need to be made.

PROOFREADING PAIRS

86. QUOTATIONS

☆ *PURPOSE*: language arts icebreaker   ☆ *AGES*: 8–adult

☆ *TIME*: 10–20 minutes

☆ *MATERIALS*: collection of famous quotations, card stock and markers (optional)

PREPARATION

Assemble a number of quotations that are suitable for your students' age and abilities. Copy each quotation onto a separate index card.

Here are a few examples:

Nobody can make you feel inferior without your consent.

   —Eleanor Roosevelt

Just because you're right doesn't mean I'm wrong.

   —Alyce Johnson

If your only tool is a hammer, you see every problem as a nail.

   —Author unknown

The only real failure is the person who doesn't even try.

   —Author unknown

Greet students at the door and give each one a quotation. Ask them to take a seat, read the quotation, and think about it for a few moments.

INSTRUCTIONS FOR STUDENTS

1. Each person has a card that contains a famous quotation. Your job is to think about the quotation and then write a brief response about what it means to you. How does it pertain to you, or to us all, as people or as learners?

2. You will have __ minutes to think about your quotation and write a response. This is not a test, and everybody earns full credit for participating.

3. This will be the signal that time is up. *[Demonstrate your Attention Getter— see the Introduction for details.]*

4. At that time, I will invite you to share your quotation and your response with the class. If you are feeling shy today, don't worry—you can give me your response and I will be your "pinch-hit reader" for today.

(continued)

QUOTATIONS

(continued)

FOLLOW-UP

Ask each student to share his or her quotation and response. Discuss each quotation as a class. Do they agree with it? Why do they think it became famous?

Invite students to copy their quotations onto card stock and illustrate them. Post them on the walls or bulletin boards to view as a class.

VARIATIONS

Instead of giving each student a different quotation, assign students to work in pairs to analyze and respond to a quotation. Invite students to share their responses.

Ask all students to write about the same quotation. Discuss their answers when they finish or collect them and read excerpts from them without identifying the authors. Give authors the option of identifying themselves. During the first days of class, many students prefer to listen to other classmates' comments without revealing their identity.

87. SIX-WORD SUMMARIES

☆ **PURPOSE**: language arts icebreaker   ☆ **AGES**: 9–adult

☆ **TIME**: 10–20 minutes

☆ **MATERIALS**: blank paper or card stock, pencils, markers

PREPARATION

Conduct a search for "six-word memoirs" on the Internet. You will find many examples and reports from teachers who have successfully used this activity for students of various ages, from elementary school to adult.

The National Public Radio website has a gallery of illustrated six-word memoirs that you can project and share with students: *www.npr.org/templates/story/story .php?storyId=18768430.*

Greet students at the door as they enter your classroom. Hand each student a piece of paper or card stock and a pencil. Ask them to take a seat and await instructions.

INSTRUCTIONS FOR STUDENTS

1 Today we're going to do an exercise in compression. First, let's take a moment to think about our lives and the many things we have experienced and accomplished.

2 Now we're going to tell our life stories—in just six words. This idea started as a project at an online magazine called *Smith*. Hundreds of people have done it, including many of my students. Here are some of theirs:

Got paddled, got smarter, got sneaky

Hated math, liked science, loved recess

Got a puppy, life got better

3 You will have ___ minutes to write your six-word summary, or memoir. Don't worry if it's not perfect. Just do your best and remember that there are no wrong answers here. We all have our own stories.

4 I have given you a pencil so you can erase words if needed, until you are happy with your memoir. Then please write it in pen or marker for easier viewing.

(continued)

FOLLOW-UP

As students finish, ask them to tack their summaries onto the board so they can be viewed as a group representing the class. It makes a nice picture and is a good conversation starter. After they are all posted, if students seem comfortable, ask them to share a little bit about their stories.

Later on, collect the memoirs and ask a student volunteer to see if he or she can distribute them to their proper owners. This is a good way to learn classmates' names.

VARIATION

If time allows, invite students to illustrate their summaries. Or they can illustrate them at a later date.

SIX-WORD SUMMARIES

88. WACKY WORDIES

☆ **PURPOSE**: language arts icebreaker   ☆ **AGES**: 7–adult

☆ **TIME**: 10–20 minutes

☆ **MATERIALS**: wordie sheets, poster board, slide show or easel paper

PREPARATION

Create a list of popular sayings or phrases that are culturally and age-appropriate, so your students are likely to be familiar with them (such as *high five, three little pigs, broken heart, coffee break,* and *buckle up*).

Draw a template on an 8.5 × 11 sheet of paper that consists of 12 two-inch squares, each with a bold black outline. Make copies of your blank template for future use.

Inside each square on the template, write words that represent a phrase, using placement, shape, and boldness of letters to give clues to the phrase. You can find many examples online with a simple search. Here are a few:

High five: print the word *five* near the top border of the box

Three little pigs: print the word *pigs* three times in small letters inside the box

Broken heart: print the word *heart* with a large space: HE~ART

Coffee break: print the word *coffee* in two parts COF~FEE

Buckle up: print the word *buckle* vertically so it is read upward

Growing older: print the word *older* with each succeeding letter a bit larger

INSTRUCTIONS FOR STUDENTS

1 We're going to use our brains in a "big-picture" way. We're going to look at some words that represent popular phrases. These are called Wacky Wordies. Here are two examples. *[Show two sample wordies.]*

2 You will have ___ minutes to see how many Wacky Wordies you can solve. This is not a test, and it's not graded. It's a brain warm-up.

FOLLOW-UP

Ask students to share their answers to the clues. Be prepared for students to come up with unexpected answers that may be correct.

Invite students to create their own Wacky Wordies as a whole group or assign them to work in pairs or teams to create new wordies for their classmates to solve.

(continued)

(continued)

VARIATIONS

For younger children, reduce the number of squares on the handout to four.

Instead of a handout, create individual posters or slides to view as a whole class, with just one wordie per poster or slide.

To increase the challenge, use phrases that are subject-specific (such as art, math, music, or science) or from the same category, such as movie or book titles or sports terms.

high five, flat broke, forever, in between jobs, coffee break, fist full of dollars (or money)

Sample Wacky Wordies

Chapter Nine

Rev Up the Reading

Literacy is the key to success in school. We know that. Without good reading comprehension, every subject becomes more difficult, and some become impossible.

Highly intelligent students cannot correctly solve math problems, for example, if they can't understand what the problem asks. So it's little wonder that programs such as DEAR (Drop Everything and Read) have become standard practice in so many schools. Teachers know from experience, and scientific research supports the anecdotal evidence, that when students get excited about reading, they learn much more quickly. In my own experience of working with reluctant and remedial readers, I learned that the key to making reading appealing and enjoyable is to find materials and activities that are so compelling that students forget they are reading. Thus, the activities in this chapter are designed to make reading fun.

Online Inspiration

I would like to recommend a website in the United Kingdom for teachers that includes hundreds of videos, including a series about literacy that my own education students rate as among the top resources for effective teaching techniques. The website address is *www.schoolsworld.tv/videos*. This resource is listed in the Appendix of this book, but I wanted to suggest specific videos for reading teachers, tutors, and administrators who are interested in schoolwide literacy improvement. In particular, I would like to recommend the series titled *Literacy: The Whole Story*, which includes sixteen fifteen-minute video clips. The first clip in the series, "Early Years: Foundation Stage Leaders", features a school that was moved out of the underachieving category not by testing, but by using games and play activities that created a love for reading and writing among the children.

89. BACK-TO-BACK

☆ **PURPOSE**: reading icebreakers   ☆ **AGES**: 6–adult

☆ **TIME**: 10–20 minutes

☆ **MATERIALS**: age-appropriate stories or easy reader books

PREPARATION

For younger students, assemble a collection of easy-to-read books. For older students, find two brief entertaining stories or articles and make copies to distribute to the class.

If your students are younger, create an area where they can sit on the floor. If you teach older students or if your chairs are attached to desks, see the suggested seating options in the next section.

Before you begin the activity, assign students to work in pairs. (See Chapter Three for quick and easy ways to randomly assign partners.) If you have an uneven number of students, participate in the partner assignment activity yourself so nobody is left out.

INSTRUCTIONS FOR STUDENTS

1. Today we're going to do an exercise called back-to-back reading. We're going to read to each other, but we are going to sit with our backs to each other. This will allow us to focus on the words and really hear them.

2. We're going to take turns. You and your partner can decide who goes first.

3. When we begin, the first person will read for ___ minutes.

4. This will be the signal that your reading time is up. *[Demonstrate your Attention Getter—see the Introduction for details.]* If you finish early, you have your choice: you can read your story again or just wait silently for the signal.

5. If you don't finish the story, don't worry. This isn't a race, and it isn't a competition. It's a listening and reading exercise to help our brains get warmed up for learning.

Suggested Seating Options: Young students can sit on the floor. Older students can place their chairs back-to-back or stand back-to-back while they read.

FOLLOW-UP

Ask for student feedback on the activity. How is reading back-to-back different from reading face-to-face? Which do they prefer?

VARIATION

Have the first student read back-to-back and the second student read face-to-face. Ask for feedback: Which did they prefer? Why?

BACK-TO-BACK

90. BOOK SWAP

☆ **PURPOSE:** reading icebreakers   ☆ **AGES:** 6–18

☆ **TIME:** 15–25 minutes

☆ **MATERIALS:** large collection of age-appropriate books, 5 × 8 index cards

PREPARATION

Assemble a collection of fiction and nonfiction books (many boys prefer nonfiction) and magazines of varying degrees of difficulty. Check books out of your school or local library or buy books at library and yard sales.

Place one book or magazine on each student desk.

Count out enough index cards for the students on your roster. In a vertical column on the left side of each index card, write the numbers 1–5.

On the board (or projected on a screen), print the following scale:

> 1 star = Hate it
>
> 2 stars = Don't really like it
>
> 3 stars = It's okay
>
> 4 stars = Pretty good
>
> 5 stars = It's a winner

Greet students as they enter the room and hand each student a numbered index card. Ask them to be seated and quietly inspect the books on their desks.

INSTRUCTIONS FOR STUDENTS

1 Today we're going to do a Book Swap in preparation for our independent reading. It's important that you find something you enjoy reading, since we'll be spending a lot of time talking and writing about what we're reading.

2 On your desk you have a book. Don't worry if it doesn't appeal to you because you are only going to read that book for two minutes. Then you will have a chance to rate it on a scale of 1 to 5. *[Show them the scale you have printed or projected.]*

3 This will be your signal that the two minutes are up. *[Demonstrate your Attention Getter.]* When you hear that sound, you will have 30 seconds to write the title of the book on your index card and give it 1 to 5 stars. Then we'll exchange books and read something else.

4 When we finish, you will have a record of book titles, along with your rating, so you will know which books you might want to read in the future.

(continued)

BOOK SWAP

(continued)

FOLLOW-UP

Repeat the activity 5 times. If time permits, repeat again with 5 different books (students will have to add numbers to their index cards). Repeat the activity on a daily basis until all students have found something they like to read.

Dana C's book ratings

1. Motorhead MaMa ★★★★★
2. Fun with Macaroni ★
3. Make My Day ★★★
4. Success Stories ★★
5. Yo! Wassup? ★★★★

Book Swap Rating Chart

91. FISHING FOR SIGHT WORDS

⭐ **PURPOSE**: reading icebreakers   ⭐ **AGES**: K-8

⭐ **TIME**: 10-20 minutes

⭐ **MATERIALS**: fishing pole, ping-pong balls, magnets, card stock and marker, pond

PREPARATION

Using a marker, write numbers on the ping-pong balls, so you have as many balls as you have students on your roster. Add a few extra numbers for unexpected arrivals. Put the numbered balls into a bag.

On card stock, print several sight words in bold letters (such as *to, the, a, an, I, me, you, we, can, dog, cat, this,* and *it*). Attach magnets to the backs of the cards.

At the end of the fishing line, attach a magnet strong enough to attract and lift the stick-on magnets on your cards.

Create a pond out of a cardboard box or a plastic tub. Paste paper or plastic fish around the perimeter of the pond.

INSTRUCTIONS FOR STUDENTS

1. Today we're going to go fishing for words. We're going to take turns.

2. First, I want everybody to come up and take a ball from the bag, without peeking. *[Distribute balls.]*

3. Whoever has number 1 will be the first fisher. Please come and get the fishing pole.

4. Now you need to cast your line into the pond and catch a word. *[Assist student as he or she fishes out a word.]* What did you catch? *[Ask student to read the card. Set the captured word aside to put back into the pond for reuse.]*

5. Who can use that word in a sentence? Please raise your hand. *[Call on volunteers.]*

6. Excellent. Now it's fisher number 2's turn to catch a word. Come on up.

FOLLOW-UP

Ask students to gather in a circle. One at a time, hold up the captured words and ask students to read them. Put all the captured words back into the pond for future use.

VARIATIONS

On butcher paper, create a series of sentences that have blanks to represent missing words. When students fish out a word, they tape it to the blank to finish the sentence.

For older students, use more difficult words or use vocabulary words.

92. I CAN SEE CLEARLY NOW

☆ **PURPOSE**: reading icebreakers   ☆ **AGES**: 6-adult

☆ **TIME**: 10–20 minutes

☆ **MATERIALS**: transparent reading filters in a variety of colors; print samples (black print on white paper); Color List handouts that list names of colors of your filters (rose, purple, blue, aqua, gray, and yellow)

PREPARATION

Research suggests that up to 50 percent of learning disabilities may stem from light sensitivity. (See Chapter Eight, on light and learning, in *Teaching Outside the Box* [Jossey-Bass, 2011].)

Find out if your school counselor is trained to test students for light sensitivity. Your school may have reading filters on hand. If not, visit two websites (*http://Irlen.com* and *www.NRSI.com*) where you can read about light sensitivity and purchase reading filters. Or, for this activity, you can use transparent notebook dividers in a variety of colors from any office supply store (normally under $5 per package).

Place print samples and 2–3 different colored transparencies at different locations in your classroom. Give each student a Color List handout.

Before you begin the activity, demonstrate your Attention Getter signal to let students know when you need their quiet attention. (See the Introduction for details.)

Divide students into groups, one group per station.

INSTRUCTIONS FOR STUDENTS

1. Today we're going to try an experiment to see if it is easier for you to read using different colors of filters. We'll spend two minutes at each station.

2. After two minutes, I will give this signal. *[Demonstrate your Attention Getter.]*

3. When you hear the signal, circle the color on your Color List that felt the best for your eyes from the colors at your station. Then we'll move to another station and try reading with different colors.

4. After you have visited all of the stations, we'll return to our seats and share our results.

FOLLOW-UP

Students may ask to use colored filters for reading (even students who are not sensitive to light). They have so much fun, they forget they are reading! Some students may find that reading with a colored filter dramatically improves their comfort and fluency. Refer those students to the counselor for light sensitivity testing—which is *not* the same as visual acuity (20-20 vision)—or recommend sensitivity testing to parents.

Students may enjoy visiting *www.NRSI.com* or *http://Irlen.com* themselves to read the research and see the examples of vision distortions.

I CAN SEE CLEARLY NOW

93. THREE-STORY VIEW

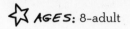

☆ *PURPOSE*: reading icebreakers   ☆ *AGES*: 8–adult

☆ *TIME*: 10–20 minutes

☆ *MATERIALS*: short stories, easel paper or butcher paper, markers

PREPARATION

Select three short age-appropriate stories. Try to find stories that are obviously different in style, tone, character development, and so on. Copy the first two pages of each story to use as student handouts.

    Before you begin the activity, assign students to work in pairs or groups. (See Chapter Three for quick and easy ways to randomly assign student work teams.)

INSTRUCTIONS FOR STUDENTS

1. We're going to look at the beginnings of three different stories.

2. How you read the stories is up to each team. You can read them silently to yourselves, or you can read them aloud to each other.

3. You will have __ minutes to read the stories. This will be your signal that the time is up. *[Demonstrate your Attention Getter—see the Introduction for details.]*

4. After you have read the stories, your mission is to discuss them with your team and come up with at least three things you think a story must have in order to have a good beginning.

5. Write your list on your paper. Please try to write legibly and large enough that we can read it from a distance.

6. So that's your mission: read the stories, discuss them, and make a list.

7. Everybody please come up and get your copy of the stories. Then move your desks and chairs to create groups where you can talk to your team without disturbing other groups. Thank you very much.

FOLLOW-UP

Assign each group to create a rubric for their criteria, apply the criteria in their rubric to the stories, and design a chart or visual aid to show their results.

    Invite each group to present their rubric and evaluations to the class. Give each group a round of applause after its presentation.

    Compare student criteria to the literary techniques and devices discussed in their textbooks: characterization, plot, setting, dialogue, and so on.

VARIATION

Allow students to create their visuals on the computer.

Taken from *Kick-Start Your Class: Academic Icebreakers to Engage Students.* Copyright © 2012 by LouAnne Johnson. Reproduced by permission of Jossey-Bass, an Imprint of Wiley. www.josseybass.com.

Chapter Ten

Social Studies Scenarios

Social studies is such an exciting and wide-ranging subject that the number of subject-related icebreakers is endless.

The activities suggested in this chapter can be adapted and revised to include dozens of different topics. For the activity Birthday Customs, instead of researching and exploring worldwide birthday customs, for example, students can investigate and share holiday celebrations, dating norms, wedding customs and costumes, breakfast foods, and so on. The activity described in World View could be designed to focus on such diverse topics as bridges, animals, churches, landscapes, footwear, bedrooms, or foods.

94. CITY SEARCH

☆ **PURPOSE:** social studies icebreaker   ☆ **AGES:** 7–adult

☆ **TIME:** 10–20 minutes

☆ **MATERIALS:** capital city template; maps, globes, atlases, dictionaries, textbooks, computer Internet

PREPARATION

Make a list of several capital cities from around the world, including those from countries unlikely to be familiar to your students (Abuja, Nigeria; Amman, Jordan; Asuncion, Paraguay; Canberra, Australia; Cardiff, Wales; Harare, Zimbabwe). Here's a good web resource: *http://geography.about.com/od/countryinformation/a/capitals.htm*.

Provide reference materials including maps, globes, atlases, dictionaries, textbooks, and computers with geographic software programs or Internet connections.

Create a template that contains a list of country names only. Leave a blank space beside each country name for students to fill in the capital city.

Before you begin the activity, assign students to work in pairs or teams. (See Chapter Three for quick and easy methods of assigning student work partners.)

INSTRUCTIONS FOR STUDENTS

1. Today we're going to be looking at some capital cities from around the world. I have made a list of countries. Each team will get a copy of the list.

2. Your mission is to find the name of the capital city for each country and write it on your list. Cities must be spelled properly in order to be considered correct.

3. You may use any of the reference materials in this room to locate the capital cities.

4. You will have __ minutes to work on your list. When the time is up, you will hear this signal. *[Demonstrate your Attention Getter—see the Introduction for details.]*

5. At that time, we will see how many capital cities each team has correctly identified.

FOLLOW-UP

Explain that the word *capitol* refers to a building, not a city.

Discuss how capital cities are chosen, and the implications and complications that can result from being selected (such as overpopulation, better employment, tourism, and political power struggles). Ask students what other cities in the United States they think would be good capitals and why.

(continued)

(continued)

VARIATIONS

Instead of listing the countries on your template, list the capital cities and let students identify the countries. Or let students create templates to exchange with classmates to see how many they can correctly identify in 10 minutes.

For younger students, use familiar countries. Instead of a template, create card sets with the country on one card and the capital city on another. Let students research and match the capitals to the countries.

CITY SEARCH

95. BIRTHDAY CUSTOMS

☆ **PURPOSE:** social studies icebreaker ☆ **AGES:** 6–16

☆ **TIME:** 10–20 minutes

☆ **MATERIALS:** balloons, marker, card stock

PREPARATION

Research birthday customs and celebrations for different countries, preferably those that will be unfamiliar to your student population. Create sets of cards for 5–10 countries. On one card, print the name of the country. On the matching card for that country, draw or glue a picture of a birthday tradition from that country (piñatas in Mexico, initiation ceremonies in Africa, noodles for lunch in China, a new outfit in Japan, birthday pies in Russia, a good-luck symbol marked on the forehead in Nepal).

Copy your card sets so you will have enough sets to give to each team in your class. Divide the number of students on your roster by 3 to get the number of teams. If you have a large class, you may opt to use 4-student teams.

Inflate one balloon for each student in your class. Number the balloons with a marker to identify them. Create slips of paper with the same numbers printed on them and put all the slips into a bag or container.

Tie a string to each balloon. Give each student a balloon as they enter the room.

INSTRUCTIONS FOR STUDENTS

1. Today we're going to explore birthday customs from around the world. But first, we're going to form our birthday teams.

2. If you have a balloon numbered 1 through ___ *(number of teams in your class)*, please come up and pull three numbers from the bag. The people who have those numbers on their balloons will be on your team.

3. Each team leader will receive a set of birthday custom cards. Your mission as a team is to match the custom with the country where that custom is practiced.

4. You will have ___ minutes to see how many customs and countries you have correctly matched.

5. This will be the signal that your time is up. *[Demonstrate your Attention Getter.]*

FOLLOW-UP

Ask students to share their family birthday customs and traditions. Discuss the importance of family and cultural traditions.

VARIATIONS

Have students create an illustrated birthday book containing birthday customs from around the world. Or design research projects related to other cultural traditions.

BIRTHDAY CUSTOMS

96. LOCAL GEOGRAPHY BINGO

☆ **PURPOSE:** social studies icebreaker   ☆ **AGES:** 6-adult

☆ **TIME:** 10-20 minutes

☆ **MATERIALS:** bingo-style cards, beans or felt-tip markers, card stock, prizes

PREPARATION

Create a list of local attractions, parks, sports teams, school names, restaurants, and businesses. Create bingo-style cards with 9-12 spaces for younger students and 20-30 for older students. Make enough cards for all the students on your roster (plus a few extras) and fill in the squares on each card randomly with topics from your list.

Copy the topics from the cards onto small squares of card stock. Place the squares into a bag or box.

Assemble a collection of small prizes (pencils, pens, gummy erasers, colorful paper clips, stickers, folders).

Greet students at the door as they enter the room. Give each student a bingo card and a handful of beans or a felt-tip marker to take to their seats.

INSTRUCTIONS FOR STUDENTS

1. We're going to play bingo, but instead of using numbers, we're going to use the names of places from our own town. These are places you may have seen or visited.

2. I will shake up the bag and draw one item. When I read the name of the person, place, or thing, look and see if you have it on your card. If you do, put a bean on that square (or make an X on that square with your marker).

3. Each time I read the name of an item, check your card. When you have __ beans (or Xs) in a row—going up, down, or diagonally (corner to corner), raise your hand and say "Bingo" to claim your prize.

FOLLOW-UP

Play the game as time permits until a few students have made bingo. If your students are very young, distribute the rest of the prizes so everybody wins one for participating and cooperating. (You might consider giving participation prizes to older students as well, even if they like to pretend they are "too cool for school.")

Assign students to create similar games using names of historical events, people, or countries from their textbooks.

VARIATION

Create bingo cards on individual whiteboards so they can be erased and reused. An online search will provide many samples. Here are two web resources: *http://www.dltk-cards.com/bingo* and *http://www.mes-english.com/flashcards/bingo.php*.

97. NAME THAT FLAG

☆ **PURPOSE:** social studies icebreaker   ☆ **AGES:** 7–adult

☆ **TIME:** 10–20 minutes

☆ **MATERIALS:** replicas of flags; maps, atlases, dictionaries, globes

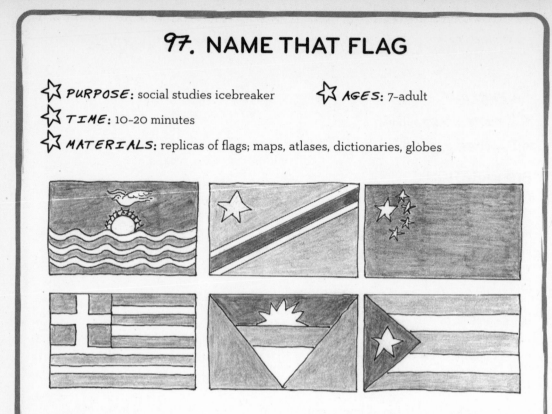

PREPARATION

This activity can be designed to refresh students' memories by using familiar flags, or to challenge them by providing unfamiliar flags.

Locate replicas of flags from around the world. If you can't find or can't afford replicas, make color copies, or quickly sketch a selection of flags using colored markers. Many dictionaries and encyclopedias include excellent reproductions.

An online search will provide many sources. Uncommon Courtesy displays a number of flags on its website, along with a template for Flags of the World Bingo, *http://www.uncommoncourtesy.com/flagsaroundtheworldbingo.htm*. And the Central Intelligence Agency (CIA) has an excellent reference on its website: *https://www.cia.gov/library/publications/the-world-factbook/docs/flagsoftheworld.html*.

Use index cards or labels to number the flags on display. The younger your students, the fewer flags you will want to use.

Before you begin the activity, assign students to work in pairs or teams. (See Chapter Three for quick and easy methods to randomly assign partners.)

Create a template with a vertical column of numbers (as many numbers as you have flags). Make a copy of the template for each pair or team of students.

(continued)

(continued)

INSTRUCTIONS FOR STUDENTS

1. Each team has a template with the name of several countries. The flags on display represent those countries.

2. Your mission is to see how many flags you can correctly identify by country.

3. You may use any of the reference materials in this room to find the answers.

4. You will have __ minutes to work on this project. When you hear this signal, it means your time is up. *[Demonstrate your Attention Getter—see the Introduction for details.]*

FOLLOW-UP

Discuss (or research) how a country's flag is chosen. Discuss the importance of color, symbols, and words in the design of a flag. Ask students why they think it is a federal crime to defile the flag. Why do some people choose to break that law?

VARIATION

Find an online quiz for students to take, such as the one at this website: *http://www.teachers.ash.org.au/jmresources/flags/flags.html.*

NAME THAT FLAG

98. STATE SILHOUETTES

☆ **PURPOSE:** social studies icebreaker   ☆ **AGES:** 7-18

☆ **TIME:** 10-20 minutes

☆ **MATERIALS:** card stock, state silhouettes

PREPARATION

Using a large U.S. map as a reference, create individual state silhouettes to scale, including Alaska and Hawaii.

Try to make silhouettes large enough that, when assembled, they will create a map that is at least five feet wide.

Glue each individual silhouette to card stock, then cut around the outline to create a puzzle piece.

Clear an area in the classroom with enough room for the puzzle to be assembled, and allow extra room for students to maneuver. If your classroom is too small, distribute the silhouettes and then take students outside to use the hallway or a common area that has little or no foot traffic—after you have given the instructions.

Greet students at the door as they enter the room and hand each student two or more puzzle pieces (depending on the number of students in your class).

INSTRUCTIONS FOR STUDENTS

1. Today, as a class, we're going to test our knowledge of U.S. geography.

2. Can anybody tell me what the silhouettes you are holding represent? *[If nobody recognizes that they are states, give them clues until they figure it out.]*

3. Your mission is to see if you can assemble the United States on the floor in less than __ minutes.

4. When you hear this signal, it means the time is up. *[Demonstrate your Attention Getter—see the Introduction for details.]*

FOLLOW-UP

Allow extra time as needed for students to finish assembling the map. Ask for volunteers to see if they can name each state. Ask students to share the names of states they have visited or where they have lived and any memorable details about landscape, weather, cultural traditions, and so on from those states.

(continued)

(continued)

VARIATIONS

Instead of silhouettes, cut individual states from a large U.S. map that includes rivers, names of states and cities, and highways. Glue each state to card stock to create a puzzle piece for students to assemble.

Instead of one large map, provide smaller individual silhouettes for students to assemble into a U.S. map on their desks or tabletops. Allow them to work in pairs.

This exercise can also be used for adult English language learners.

99. OUR WORLD MAP

☆ **PURPOSE**: social studies icebreaker   ☆ **AGES**: 7–adult

☆ **TIME**: 10–20 minutes

☆ **MATERIALS**: world map, multicolored sticky notes

PREPARATION

Find or make a replica of a world map that is large enough to be seen from a distance. Place a sticky note on the map to mark the places you have lived in or visited, where your ancestors lived, or where you now have friends or family. Provide each student with a small supply of sticky notes.

INSTRUCTIONS FOR STUDENTS

1. Today we're going to discover the connections of the people in our class to the world.

2. First, take a minute to think about where your ancestors lived, if you know that information. Let's also think about where any friends or family may live now. Or think of places that you may have lived or visited, including places in the United States. *[Pause for thinking.]*

3. I have already placed my stickers on the map. *[Point to each sticker and explain why you placed it there.]*

4. Okay. Now I would like you to write your name or the name of your relative or friend on a sticky note and place it in the right location on the map. If you aren't exactly sure where a place is, we'll help you find it.

5. Let's write the names on our stickers. And as soon as you are ready, go ahead and stick them on the map.

If students are hesitant, invite them individually to approach the map and place their stickers.

FOLLOW-UP

Ask students to identify the sticky notes they have attached to the map and explain who they know that lives or has lived in those countries. Ask students to share their travel experiences. If they haven't traveled, ask them what places they would like to visit.

VARIATIONS

If appropriate for your class, use a U.S. map instead of a world map. And use multicolored pushpins instead of sticky notes.

Give students individual world map or U.S. map outlines and ask them to draw Xs or stars to indicate any locations they have lived or visited, where their ancestors lived, or where they now have friends or family.

100. TIME STRETCHERS

⭐ **PURPOSE**: social studies icebreaker   ⭐ **AGES**: 11–adult

⭐ **TIME**: 10–20 minutes

⭐ **MATERIALS**: index cards or card stock, markers

PREPARATION

Create a timeline for a specific historical period (era, decade, century) that includes a chronological list of specific events: conflicts, theories, discoveries, cultural icons, influential personalities, laws established or changed, or important court cases.

For each event on your list, create an individual 5 × 8 index card with a brief description of the people, places, or things involved. In bold marker, give each event card a unique title. Mark an X on the backs of the first and last event cards in the timeline.

Once you have a complete set of event cards, make enough copies to give a complete set to each student team. To avoid confusion, you can create different-colored sets by copying the original cards on pastel paper. Glue the pastel paper cards to card stock to make them more durable. Mark the backs of the first and last cards in each set with Xs.

Before you begin the activity, assign students to work in pairs or teams. (See Chapter Three for quick and easy methods of assigning random partners.)

INSTRUCTIONS FOR STUDENTS

1 I'm going to give each team a set of cards that list events that occurred between ___ and ___ [insert years or other time period].

2 Your mission is to place those cards in the correct chronological order, according to when the events took place. You will find Xs on the back of the first and last events.

3 You may use your textbook or other reference materials in this room to complete your timelines.

4 You will have __ minutes to work on your timeline. When you hear this signal, it means your time is up. [Demonstrate your Attention Getter.]

FOLLOW-UP

Discuss the individual events in the timeline. Ask for student input about their associations with or knowledge of each event.

Stretch the timeline by presenting additional events that are not in the original card set. Ask students to place the new events in their historical context.

VARIATIONS

Delete the Xs on the first and last event cards to increase the challenge. Or have students create their own personal timelines, from their birth to the present.

101. WORLD VIEW

☆ *PURPOSE:* social studies icebreaker   ☆ *AGES:* 7–adult

☆ *TIME:* 10–20 minutes

☆ *MATERIALS:* pictures or slides from around the world

PREPARATION

Assemble a collection of pictures or slides of people, costumes, animals, famous statues, landscapes, and cityscapes from around the world. For younger students, select familiar scenes with an occasional challenger. Increase the challenge for older students by including unfamiliar locations or close-ups of parts of objects such as a face from a painting or the hat from a costume.

For the last slide, use a picture of your school.

Number the pictures or slides to identify them.

Create a numbered template, with one number for each picture in your collection. Leave a blank space beside each number for students to fill in. Make copies of the template to distribute to students.

Before you begin the activity, assign students to work in pairs. (See Chapter Three for quick and easy methods of randomly assigning partners.)

INSTRUCTIONS FOR STUDENTS

1 I am going to show you pictures (or slides) of some people, animals, and scenes from around the world. I will identify each picture (or slide) by number.

2 Your mission is to identify, after discussing it with your partner, the country where the city, person, animal, landscape, or object can be found.

3 You will have __ minutes (or seconds) to discuss each picture. When the time is up, you will hear this signal. *[Demonstrate your Attention Getter.]*

FOLLOW-UP

Present each picture or slide and ask students to identify its country. Be prepared for students to offer correct answers that may not be on your list. Discuss each picture or slide and ask students for any personal association with or knowledge about it.

VARIATIONS

Provide individual handouts with photos of various scenes from around the world. See how many students can identify them on their own or with a partner.

For young students, use scenes from their town or from inside your own school, such as the library or the attendance office, instead of scenes from around the world.

Chapter Eleven

Techno Tasks

As a formerly low-tech woman who has recently moved up to the mid-tech category, I realize that keeping up with the latest electronic technology is impossible.

It seems that no sooner do I learn how to operate a gadget than it is now considered obsolete and has been replaced by a newer, smaller, faster, smarter gadget. But public schools tend to be like many of us older teachers—a decade or so behind the wave of advancing technology. So the activities in this chapter rely on old-fashioned computers, scanners, and digital cameras. No doubt, younger and more techno-savvy teachers will have plenty of tweaks and changes to make, especially teachers who enjoy the luxury of interactive walls and boards in their classrooms. And I hope those savvy teachers will post their favorite icebreakers online to inspire and guide the rest of us.

102. ADD A SENTENCE

⭐ **PURPOSE:** technology icebreaker   ⭐ **AGES:** 6-16

⭐ **TIME:** 10-30 minutes

⭐ **MATERIALS:** computer with word-processing software

PREPARATION

Create a document that contains just the first sentence of a story. Copy the document onto student desktops.

Before you begin the activity, assign students to work in pairs. Also, demonstrate your Attention Getter—see the Introduction for details.

INSTRUCTIONS FOR STUDENTS

1. On your desktop you will find the first sentence of a story. We're going to finish the story, sentence by sentence.

2. When I give the signal to start, your mission is to type the next sentence of the story.

3. You will have __ seconds (or minutes) to write your sentence. Then I will give the signal that time is up. *[Demonstrate your Attention Getter again.]*

4. When you hear the signal, save your story. Then move to the next computer.

5. At each computer, your job is to add the next sentence. And we'll see where these stories take us.

6. After ten rounds, we will print out the stories and I'll ask for volunteers to read them to the class.

FOLLOW-UP

Print out student lists or stories and post them on the bulletin board. Save them for future use in proofreading, editing, revising, and other writing assignments.

To increase the challenge, ask students to add a graphic, or multiple graphics, to the story at some point. Or add a different requirement for each round: add a title to the story; enlarge the font of the title and make it boldface; change the color of the font for the title; italicize the main character's name wherever it appears.

VARIATIONS

If your students are younger, have them create a list of words instead of writing sentences. Provide a prompt such as Things I Would Take on a Trip to Mars or Things I Know How to Do. For each round, they add one thing to the list.

You can also have younger students type a word from a spelling list for each round. The teacher pronounces the word, and the students type it onto a list.

ADD A SENTENCE

162

103. MAP YOUR SCHOOL

☆ **PURPOSE:** technology icebreaker ☆ **AGES:** 7–adult

☆ **TIME:** 15–30 minutes

☆ **MATERIALS:** computer with graphics software

PREPARATION

Prepare instructions for this activity as a document or slideshow presentation. Include specific criteria such as required design elements, animations, and a deadline for completion. Copy the instruction sheet to student desktops or present a slideshow to the entire class before starting the assignment—or do both to ensure better understanding.

Before beginning the activity, assign students to work in pairs. (See Chapter Three for quick and easy methods of assigning work partners.)

INSTRUCTIONS FOR STUDENTS

1 Your assignment today is to create a map of our school. Complete instructions for this assignment appear in the document on your desktop. Please locate that now.

2 We will be using the Three Before Me policy during this assignment. That means you need to do three things before you ask me for help: first, check the online Help database; second, check the instruction manual; and, third, ask a classmate.

3 If those three options fail, then ask me. This policy is meant to help you learn to be independent learners. I am happy to help you, but I want to be sure that you can help yourself when an instructor is not available.

4 You will have __ minutes to work on this project. If you don't finish today, you will have an opportunity to work on this later in the week.

FOLLOW-UP

Print out student maps and post them in various locations throughout the school (you may need to request administrative approval). If possible, enlarge the maps and laminate them.

Ask students to vote for the best map. Submit it to the school administration for use on the school website or informational publications.

VARIATIONS

Limit the assignment. Instead of mapping the entire school, have students map their classroom. Or expand the assignment to include mapping their town. Add or subtract requirements according to student age and ability levels.

104. SELL A SUBJECT

⭐ **PURPOSE**: technology icebreaker ⭐ **AGES**: 7-adult
⭐ **TIME**: 15-30 minutes
⭐ **MATERIALS**: computers with word-processing software

PREPARATION

Create an instruction sheet that outlines the requirements for this assignment. Store the sheet as a document on student desktops or make paper copies to distribute to students.

Before you begin the activity, assign students to work in pairs. (See Chapter Three for quick and easy methods of assigning work partners.)

INSTRUCTIONS FOR STUDENTS

1 Today your assignment is to create a one-page flyer with graphics to "sell" a school subject to students. You can choose a general subject such as math or physical education, or you can select a specific course such as geometry or soccer.

2 You will find specific criteria on the assignment sheet, but basically your project needs to be visually appealing, informative, and persuasive. Why should somebody study the subject you are selling?

3 You will have ___ minutes to work on your projects. This will be your signal that the time is up. *[Demonstrate your Attention Getter—see the Introduction for details.]*

4 Feel free to help each other. And we're going to use the Three Before Me policy. Before you ask me for help, you need to search for Help on the computer, look in a user guide, and ask a classmate. If those three things fail to help you, then I'll be happy to see if I can help you find a solution.

FOLLOW-UP

Teams print out their flyers and take turns presenting them to the class. Classmates provide written or verbal peer critiques, citing two things they liked and one thing that could be improved.

VARIATIONS

Expand the topic to include nonacademic subjects, such as skateboarding or playing video games.

If time permits and students are experienced computer users, have them create trifold brochures or digital slideshows instead of flyers.

105. WHAT WE KNOW SLIDESHOW

☆ **PURPOSE**: technology icebreaker   ☆ **AGES**: 7–adult

☆ **TIME**: 15–30 minutes

☆ **MATERIALS**: computers with slideshow presentation software

PREPARATION

Create an instruction sheet that outlines the requirements for this assignment. Store the sheet as a document on student desktops or distribute paper copies to students after you assign work partners or teams. (If you give people something to read, many of them will tune you out, even if you ask them to wait until you are finished talking before they begin reading.)

INSTRUCTIONS FOR STUDENTS

1. Today your assignment is to create a slideshow on the topic What We Know About ___ *[insert any topic: biology, geography, osmosis, puppies, school, wolves . . .].*

2. Your slideshow should have between ___ and ___ slides *[insert numbers suitable for the age and ability of your students].*

3. Other requirements, such as graphics, animation, and transitions, are outlined on the assignment sheet on your desktop *[or you may distribute assignment sheets now].*

4. You will have ___ minutes to work on your slideshow. This will be your signal that time is up. *[Demonstrate your Attention Getter—see the Introduction for details.]*

5. Don't worry if you don't finish it all right now. You will have time to work on these later.

6. Feel free to help each other. And we're going to use the Three Before Me policy: before you ask me for help, you need to search for Help on the computer, look in a user guide, and ask a classmate. If those three things fail to help you, then I'll be happy to see if I can help you find a solution.

FOLLOW-UP

Roam around the room, offering encouragement, praise, and assistance as needed. As students finish, view their slideshows. If time permits, or at a later time, let each team present its slideshow to the class.

VARIATION

Instead of assigning the topic for the slideshow, let students choose their topics.

106. WORDLE TEAMS

⭐ **PURPOSE:** technology icebreaker

⭐ **AGES:** 7–adult

⭐ **TIME:** 10–20 minutes

⭐ **MATERIALS:** computers with Internet access

PREPARATION

Visit the Wordle web page (*www.wordle.net*) to familiarize yourself with the program. Search online for lesson plans using Wordle. A good place to start is at *http://www.ideastoinspire.co.uk/wordle.htm*. This site is titled "51 Interesting Ways to Use Wordle in the Classroom." (Categories include writing, spelling, Internet safety, early years, science, geography, math, homework, and music.)

INSTRUCTIONS FOR STUDENTS

1. Go to the Wordle home page: *www.wordle.net*.

2. Click on the word "Create," which will open a window.

3. Inside the first box type a few statements about yourself. What are your favorite school subjects? What are your hobbies? Favorite foods? Names of friends, family, and pets?

4. After you have typed your comments, click "Go." Wordle will create a word cloud for you.

5. Click on "Randomize" to see different arrangements.

6. You will have ___ minutes to create your word cloud. I will give you a one-minute warning so you can finish up.

(continued)

(continued)

FOLLOW-UP

Let students walk around and view each other's pages.

As a future class project, have the students create a slideshow featuring their individual word pages or using material they have studied in class.

VARIATIONS

Have students type in text from an article or a passage in their textbooks to create new word clouds.

If you only have one computer in your classroom, have students work in teams. While one team uses the computer, other teams can prepare lists or text that they will use when it's their turn. Assign students a task to complete after they create and print their word clouds: laminate them and post them on the wall, analyze them to see which words appeared most frequently, or prepare another list or text sample to compare with the first word cloud.

use with I-Pads for Station Rotation

Chapter Twelve

Artistic Experiences

Art is such an important aspect of people's lives—often an unrecognized aspect, although color and design are priorities in our choices of clothing, home decor, even food.

And despite declining budgets in most districts, schools continue to support the arts, and teachers continue to incorporate art into their lessons across the curriculum. If your school board or administrators suffer from art aversion, I highly recommend showing them the video clip "Do Schools Kill Creativity?" featuring a talk by Sir Ken Robinson. The speech can be found on YouTube or TED Talks by doing a simple online search.

Addressing "Art Anxiety"

Art is fun. Sadly, though, some students become upset by any art-related activity. Just as many students consider themselves "math challenged," many also believe they lack any artistic ability whatsoever. They have been traumatized by negative responses to their art during elementary or secondary school. Even successful, intelligent adults may become agitated or anxious when you assign any art-related project (one of my adult students who turned out to be quite talented referred to them as "artsy-crafty-torture activities" until she realized that she wasn't going to be graded or judged on her artistic abilities).

Provide gentle encouragement and make sure they realize that for the purpose of this activity, there is no "bad art." If you decide to use an art icebreaker in a nonart class, you may have students who protest loudly or adamantly refuse to participate. If that happens, appoint those frightened students to serve as art consultants or teacher assistants during the project. Or sit down and work with them yourself, side by side, to provide encouragement and assistance. Keep in mind that refusal to participate in art projects usually stems from a fear of failure and not from lack of creativity.

107. ANIMAL FIGURINES

☆ **PURPOSE**: art icebreaker   ☆ **AGES**: 6–adult

☆ **TIME**: 10–30 minutes

☆ **MATERIALS**: self-drying modeling clay

PREPARATION

Create two sample animal figurines of your own—one real and one imaginary.

INSTRUCTIONS FOR STUDENTS

1. Let's take a moment to think about some of our favorite animals and imaginary creatures, such as unicorns or hobbits.

2. Choose one of your favorites and mentally create a picture of this animal or creature. Picture the shape of its head and body. What kind of feet does it have? Does it have a tail? If so, is it bushy or thin? Straight or curly?

3. Now we're going to create our favorite animals using clay. Here are two of my favorites. *[Present your samples and explain why you chose those animals.]*

4. We'll have __ minutes to create our figurines. They don't have to be perfect, and this isn't a contest—everybody earns full credit for participating.

5. As you are creating your figurine, think about why you chose that particular animal. Why does it appeal to you? Because of its beauty? Intelligence? Power? Special talents?

FOLLOW-UP

If students seem shy, invite them to walk around the room to admire and discuss each other's figurines. If students seem comfortable, invite them to share their figurines and explain why they chose their animals (for example, bears are strong, dogs are loyal, or birds are free).

Use this activity as a springboard for other activities. For example, if a student says she chose to create a bird figure because birds are free, assign students the task of creating a drawing that depicts or represents "freedom."

VARIATION

Instead of creating animal figurines, have students create figurines of themselves, a favorite pet, or someone in their family.

108. ARTISTS & ART

☆ **PURPOSE:** art icebreaker ☆ **AGES:** 5–adult

☆ **TIME:** 10–25 minutes, depending on age and number of students

☆ **MATERIALS:** samples of famous art pieces, card stock, index cards

PREPARATION

Assemble a collection of reproductions of famous paintings, sculptures, and art installations. Glue each reproduction to a piece of card stock and print the name of the artist on an index card, so you have created a matching set of cards for each image. Locate photos of all the artists and add a third card to each set by gluing each artist's photo to another index card.

Count the number of students on your roster and divide by three to get the number of card sets you will need. If the number isn't divisible by three, give one or two students two cards each so they will form two pairs among your three-person teams.

As students enter the room, hand each one an art reproduction, an artist photo card, or an artist name card.

INSTRUCTIONS FOR STUDENTS

1. You are holding a reproduction of a piece of art or a card bearing an artist's name or a photograph of an artist.

2. Your task is to match your card with the two other people who have cards pertaining to the same artist.

3. You will have __ minutes to locate your partners.

4. When you have located your partners, your next task is to answer the following three questions about your artist and his or her art:

→ What do you think might have inspired this particular piece?

→ How do you think people respond to this piece when they first see it?

→ If you were museum curators, would you display this piece? Why or why not?

FOLLOW-UP

Invite each team to display its art to the class and share its answers to the three questions. Offer the options of appointing spokespeople or answering together as a team if they need moral support.

(continued)

(continued)

VARIATIONS

For young students, use familiar storybook and cartoon characters (such as Snow White or Winnie the Pooh) and print the name of each character on a card to create matching sets.

Nonreaders can ask the teacher or aide to read the names on the character cards to help them find their matches. Their partner question to discuss and answer is: What do you think about this picture? What does it make you think about?

109. HEAD & SHOULDERS

⭐ **PURPOSE:** art icebreaker   ⭐ **AGES:** 5-adult

⭐ **TIME:** 10-20 minutes

⭐ **MATERIALS:** butcher paper, pencils, markers

PREPARATION

Cut butcher paper into sections. In one corner of each sheet, using a bold marker, write a number in sequence, beginning with 1. Repeat each number on two different sheets so you will have enough matching pairs for all the students on your roster. If the number of students is uneven, the teacher or aide will need to participate.

Create your own head-and-shoulders outline and color in your hair, face, and clothing. Write words or draw pictures to depict a favorite hobby and a favorite pet.

Before you distribute the butcher paper, demonstrate your Attention Getter signal, so students will know what to expect. (See the Introduction for details.)

Give each student a piece of butcher paper and a pencil.

INSTRUCTIONS FOR STUDENTS

1. You have two jobs today. Your first job is to find the number in the corner of your paper. When I say, "Go," you will have __ minutes to find the partner who has the same number on his or her paper as you have on yours.

2. Does everybody see his or her number? Okay. Ready? Go. *[Use your Attention Getter to signal when the time is up.]*

3. Excellent. Now I'm going to give everybody a pencil. Please print your name beside the number on your paper. *[Wait for students to write their names.]*

4. Next we're going to take turns lying down on our backs on top of our papers. Your partner will trace around your head and shoulders with a pencil. *[Demonstrate how to do this.]*

5. Then, after you both have your outlines traced, you can use markers to go over the lines and make them darker. Then you can add your face and hair and clothes. *[Demonstrate how to do this.]*

6. The last thing you will add to your paper is a picture of a favorite hobby or pet. Here's what your finished picture will look like. *[Display your completed outline.]*

FOLLOW-UP

Hang the finished outlines on the wall to create a "class photo." Invite students to browse and discuss each other's outlines.

VARIATION

Provide a generic human outline on a template instead of having students trace heads and shoulders themselves.

110. "ME" COLLAGE

☆ **PURPOSE:** art icebreaker   ☆ **AGES:** 6–adult

☆ **TIME:** 10–20 minutes

☆ **MATERIALS:** poster board or card stock, odds and ends, scissors, glue sticks, markers, paint and brushes (optional), wire cutters (optional)

PREPARATION

Provide a piece of poster board (for larger collages) or a sheet of 8.5 × 11 card stock (for small collages) for each student on your roster.

Assemble a collection of objects and odds and ends that can be glued to poster board (such as buttons, pieces of cloth, wire, string, yarn, metal washers, old magazines and calendars, pipe cleaners, sequins, colorful toothpicks, packaging "popcorn," cotton balls, plastic eyes with movable pupils, rubber-covered paper clips, multicolored sticky notes, construction paper, tinfoil, small toys, beans, and macaroni).

Create your own collage to use as a sample.

INSTRUCTIONS FOR STUDENTS

1 Instead of introducing ourselves verbally, we're going to create collages that represent our personalities. There is no right or wrong way to create a collage. The only requirement is that you incorporate your first name into your collage in some way.

2 You may use any of the materials available in this room. Please share the glue sticks, scissors, and other tools.

3 You'll have __ minutes to create your collage. When you hear this signal, it means you have two minutes to finish up. [Demonstrate your Attention Getter—see the Introduction for details.]

FOLLOW-UP

Display the completed collages on desktops or hang them on the wall and invite students to browse and discuss them.

Many students are shy on the first day of class and may prefer not to present their collages. But if you have an outgoing class, invite students to share their collages individually and explain the different components.

VARIATIONS

Instead of creating collages that represent their personalities, ask students to create a collage that represents school. Or let them choose their own subjects.

"ME" COLLAGE

111. PARTNER SILHOUETTES

⭐ **PURPOSE:** art icebreaker   ⭐ **AGES:** 6–adult

⭐ **TIME:** 10–20 minutes

⭐ **MATERIALS:** ping-pong balls, spotlight(s) or flashlights, butcher paper, pencils, crayons or markers, odds and ends

PREPARATION

Assemble a collection of lightweight odds and ends that can be glued to paper without weighing it down too much (such as cotton balls, yarn, pipe cleaners, toothpicks, sequins, glitter, and recycled foam "peanut" packing materials).

Cut butcher paper into large sections, one for each student on your roster. Working with a partner, create your own silhouette to display as a sample. Make your sample age-appropriate so students will be able to use it as a model, if necessary.

Shine spotlight(s) onto a wall where students can hang the butcher paper and stand in front of it to create their silhouettes. Or provide several flashlights.

Paint different colored designs on the ping-pong balls, creating two of each design to be used to identify student work partners. Place all the balls in a bag.

Greet students as they enter the room, and invite each one to draw a ping-pong ball from the bag.

INSTRUCTIONS FOR STUDENTS

1. Your first task today will be to locate your partner by finding the person whose ping-pong ball has the same design as yours.

2. Next we'll be drawing our silhouettes. You can be bold and use a marker—or you can trace the silhouette using a pencil and then go over the lines with marker.

3. After we have traced our silhouettes, we're going to personalize them. You can use paint, markers, crayons, or any of the materials available in the supply area. Here is my own personalized silhouette. *[Display your sample silhouette.]*

4. You'll have __ minutes to work on this project. When you hear this signal, it means you have two minutes left to finish up. *[Demonstrate your Attention Getter—see the Introduction for details.]*

(continued)

PARTNER SILHOUETTES

176

(continued)

FOLLOW-UP

Post the silhouettes on the wall and see if students can correctly identify their classmates. Invite them to browse and discuss their creations.

VARIATIONS

If time is an issue, reserve Step 3 of the preceding instructions for completion at a later date.

Print the names of various strong emotions on index cards (such as love, hate, fear, anger, and jealousy). Give each student pair an index card and the task of creating silhouettes that represent the emotion on the card.

112. NEWSPAPER HATS

☆ **PURPOSE**: art icebreaker   ☆ **AGES**: 6–adult

☆ **TIME**: 10–20 minutes

☆ **MATERIALS**: old newspapers, tape (optional)

PREPARATION

Create at least two different newspaper hats to display as samples. Begin by creating a band that will fit around your forehead. Build your hat from there.

If you have the personality to carry it off, wear one of your hats as you introduce the activity.

This may sound like a silly activity, and it is a bit silly, but I have observed it done with a group of adults who thoroughly enjoyed themselves after they whined and moaned about how impossible it was to create a hat out of just newspapers. They made towering hats, hats with braids, and hats with ears and horns and antennae.

INSTRUCTIONS FOR STUDENTS

1. Your task today is to create a hat using just newspapers. Once you get started, you'll be surprised how many different shapes you can make. You can create ears, braids, antennae, horns, tentacles, and shapes of your own design.

2. We'll have __ minutes to make our hats. When your hear this signal, it means you have two minutes left to finish up your hat. *[Demonstrate your Attention Getter—see the Introduction for details.]*

3. Feel free to help each other, if a classmate asks for advice or assistance.

4. Okay. Let's begin. Help yourself to as much newspaper as you think you'll need. You can always get more paper if you find that you need more.

FOLLOW-UP

If students seem receptive, start a newspaper hat parade moving around the classroom, so everybody can see each other's hats. Or go around the room and ask each student to explain what his or her hat represents.

VARIATIONS

Provide tape if using newspaper alone is too difficult for students.

Instead of paper hats, ask older students to create something else from the newspapers—an abstract form that represents education or life in some way, for example.

113. TINFOIL SCULPTURES

☆ **PURPOSE:** art icebreaker   ☆ **AGES:** 7–adult

☆ **TIME:** 10–20 minutes

☆ **MATERIALS:** tinfoil (clean and recycled, if possible), index cards, markers, tape

PREPARATION

Collect sufficient tinfoil to give each student enough to form a small animal sculpture.

Create two sample sculptures of your own, one real and one imaginary.

Greet students as they enter the room and give each one some tinfoil, an index card, and a marker.

INSTRUCTIONS FOR STUDENTS

1. Your assignment is to create an animal using only tinfoil. Your animal can be real or imaginary, such as a monster or a unicorn or something of your own invention.

2. When you are finished, please print your name at the bottom of the index card and tape your animal to the top of the card so your name is visible.

3. If you want to give your animal a name, too, please do.

4. You will have ___ minutes to create your animal. This will be the signal that you have ___ minutes to finish up. *[Demonstrate your Attention Getter— see the Introduction for details.]*

FOLLOW-UP

Roam around the classroom, offering encouragement. As students finish their animals, the teacher asks them to explain what that particular animal means to them.
    Have students create a display for their animals and let them browse and discuss each other's creations.

VARIATION

Instead of assigning animal sculptures, allow students to choose the object they would like to create. Ask classmates to see if they can identify each sculpture. Invite students to discuss their creations if they want to. If they don't wish to, allow them to observe.

TINFOIL SCULPTURES

114. WINDOW ON MY WORLD

☆ **PURPOSE:** art icebreaker   ☆ **AGES:** 6–adult

☆ **TIME:** 10–20 minutes

☆ **MATERIALS:** empty cereal boxes, glue sticks, markers, paint and brushes

PREPARATION

Provide an empty cereal box (or boxes of different sizes) for each student on your roster. Cut off the front of each box, leaving the sides intact to create a "window box."

Assemble a collection of lightweight odds and ends that can be glued easily to cardboard (such as buttons, pieces of cloth, string, yarn, pictures from old magazines and calendars, pipe cleaners, sequins, toothpicks, cotton balls, construction paper, tinfoil, facial tissue, and paper streamers).

Create your own window box to display as a sample. Use paint to create a frame around your box so that when hung on the wall, it will give the illusion that you are looking into a window. Include your name somewhere in your window.

INSTRUCTIONS FOR STUDENTS

1. Your mission today is to create a window into your world. You can portray yourself at home, at school, or doing something you enjoy such as a sport or hobby. Here's my window. *[Display your window and explain its contents.]*

2. You can select your own box from the ones that I have collected for you.

3. What you choose to show is up to you. The only requirement is that you include your first name somewhere in your window. And, of course, you need to keep it clean.

4. You may use any of the materials available in this room. Please share. And if you need something that you can't find, please let me know.

5. You'll have __ minutes to create your window view. When you hear this signal, it will mean you have two minutes to finish up. *[Demonstrate your Attention Getter—see the Introduction for details.]*

FOLLOW-UP

Tack the finished boxes to the wall and invite students to go "window shopping" and discuss the various views.

Many students feel shy or nervous on the first day of school, so they appreciate not having to stand up in front of peers. But if your class seems comfortable, invite them to share and discuss their windows. Let them opt to just observe, if they don't want to talk.

(continued)

(continued)

VARIATIONS

Instead of creating windows that represent themselves, ask students to create windows that show their families, pets, or favorite hobbies. Or let them choose their own subjects.

Sample Window on My World

Chapter Thirteen

Musical Moments

Music can be a powerful teaching tool. Everybody has an internal beat to which they resonate. And music in the classroom, in any form, will generate an enthusiastic response from students, especially younger children who haven't learned to hide their delight or judge their dancing abilities.

Teachers of nonmusical academic subjects can take advantage of people's natural affinity for music by using these icebreakers and by incorporating music into their lessons and classrooms. Teachers may use different kinds of music to signal quiet writing time, cleanup time, social time, the beginning or end of specific activities, and so on.

A number of websites offer songs created especially for classrooms, and other sites suggest ways to use rhythm and music to generate student interest in learning activities. Following are a few music-related websites that are not included in the Appendix:

To hear biology professor Eric Simon (a lead author with Pearson Education) discuss his use of music in his teaching, view his YouTube video at *http://www.youtube.com/watch?v=sczj2mYvmTo*.

Classroom Compass is an online publication by the Southwest Educational Development Laboratory. Their fall 1998 issue is titled *Teaching Math with Music* and can be found online at *http://www.sedl.org/scimath/compass/v04n02*.

Teachers can find lesson plan ideas for teaching math operations through songs at *http://lth3.k12.il.us/rhampton/mi/lessonplanideas.htm#Musical/Rhythmic%20Intelligence*.

115. BEATS ME

⭐ **PURPOSE:** music icebreaker   ⭐ **AGES:** 7–adult

⭐ **TIME:** 10–20 minutes

⭐ **MATERIALS:** index cards, music samples

PREPARATION

Create a set of index cards with the name of one dance beat per card—such as cha-cha, waltz, samba, polka, tango, and foxtrot (and the two-step in rural areas). Duplicate your card set so you have one for each pair or team of students.

As students enter the room, give each one an index card.

Before you begin the activity, demonstrate your Attention Getter (see the Introduction for details), which you will use to quickly get students' attention for the next step.

INSTRUCTIONS FOR STUDENTS

1 First we're going to form teams. You have __ seconds (or minutes) to locate the classmate(s) who has (or have) the same dance beat written on his or her card. Go. *[Use your Attention Getter to signal the end of the time.]*

2 Now we're going to review the different dance rhythms. Who can tap out a waltz beat? *[Choose a volunteer or do it yourself if students are shy. Repeat with each of the different beats you have included in this activity.]*

3 Okay, now that our memories are refreshed, we're going to test them. I'm going to play a musical selection. As soon as you can identify the beat, hold up the card that has that beat printed on it.

(continued)

(continued)

FOLLOW-UP

Discuss the origin of various dances. How do people create a dance rhythm? Invite student teams to invent a new dance beat (they may also opt to design the steps to accompany their beat). Share the beats (and associated dance steps) with the class.

VARIATIONS

Ask drummers to identify and play beats such as paradiddle or flimflam.

For more advanced music students, use cards with words such as *syncopated*, *adagio*, *forte*, and *pianissimo* and play samples for them to identify.

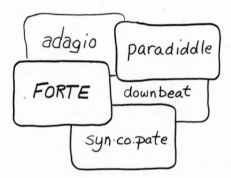

116. MUSIC-PICTURE MATCH

☆ **PURPOSE**: music icebreaker   ☆ **AGES**: 7–adult

☆ **TIME**: 10–20 minutes

☆ **MATERIALS**: collection of pictures, various musical selections

PREPARATION

Assemble a large collection of pictures, illustrations, and abstract art. Pages from old art magazines or books (which you can buy at Friends of the Library sales) work well for this activity.

Create a series of musical selections with distinctly different rhythm instruments and/or tones.

INSTRUCTIONS FOR STUDENTS

1. Music can evoke emotions and memories and visions. Today we're going to think about what we "see" and what kind of images different music can make.

2. Here is a selection of pictures. *[Place the pictures in various locations around the room, spreading them out across a wide area.]*

3. I'm going to play __ seconds (or minutes) of some different songs. Your challenge is to select a picture to match the song before the music stops.

4. After each song, I'll ask for volunteers to share the pictures they selected and explain why they chose them.

FOLLOW-UP

Switch the activity around. Project a picture on a screen or hold up a picture that is large enough for everybody to see clearly. Give students a few minutes to come up with a short melody or a beat to match the picture.

VARIATION

Provide paper and markers or pencils instead of pictures and ask students to draw what they "see" when they hear each musical selection.

117. MUSICAL MOODS

☆ **PURPOSE:** music icebreaker   ☆ **AGES:** 7-adult

☆ **TIME:** 10-20 minutes

☆ **MATERIALS:** music, paper and pens or pencils, or dry-erase markers and board

PREPARATION

Create a series of short excerpts (30-90 seconds each) of songs that have distinctly different melodies, rhythms, and tones.

Greet students at the door as they arrive. Give each student a few sheets of paper and a pencil or pen. Play music softly as students take their seats.

INSTRUCTIONS FOR STUDENTS

1 Before we begin our listening activity, I'd like to know what kind of mood the music that is playing evokes. How does this music make you feel? What kind of mood does it create? *[Discuss.]*

2 Now we're going to listen to some different musical excerpts. While the music is playing, pay attention to how the music makes you feel. Each selection will last __ seconds (or minutes).

3 While the music is playing, write down as many words as you can that describe the feelings or mood that the music creates.

4 After the music ends, I'll ask for volunteers to share what they wrote. Don't worry, you don't have to volunteer. And there is no right or wrong answer. Listening to music is a personal experience; we all bring our own experiences with us, and we all take something different from hearing each song.

FOLLOW-UP

Assign students to work in small groups. (See Chapter Three for quick and easy ways to randomly assign student work teams.) Repeat the activity (with different music) and challenge each group to come up with 20 words to describe each musical selection.

VARIATION

Instead of using paper and pencils, invite students to write their feelings on a large dry-erase board while the music is playing. Each student can write multiple feelings. After the music stops, ask for volunteers to discuss their contributions. (If you don't have a dry-erase or whiteboard, use a large sheet of butcher paper for each song.)

118. WHAT COLOR IS THIS SONG?

☆ **PURPOSE**: music icebreaker ☆ **AGES**: 7–adult

☆ **TIME**: 10–20 minutes

☆ **MATERIALS**: music, paper and pens or pencils, paint charts or color wheels

PREPARATION

Locate several color wheels or sample color charts, such as the type hardware stores use to make the formula for various paint colors—or create your own large color chart by mixing different colors and painting a large blob of each color on a poster, along with a unique name for each color.

Create a series of short excerpts (30–60 seconds each) of a variety of songs, some familiar to your students, others that will sound new.

Greet students at the door and give each one a few sheets of paper and a pencil or pen. Play music softly as they take their seats.

INSTRUCTIONS FOR STUDENTS

1. Before we begin our listening activity, let's all close our eyes and listen to the song that is playing. And let's see what colors this song brings to mind. Let's listen for about 15 or 20 seconds without talking. *[Pause to listen.]*

2. What colors come to mind when you hear this music? *[Ask volunteers to share. Discuss their answers.]*

3. Now we're going to listen to some different musical excerpts. While the music is playing, pay attention to the sound, the feeling, and the loudness. You may want to close your eyes. That's up to you. I will play each song for __ seconds.

4. While the song is playing, please write down any colors that come to mind as you listen.

5. After the music ends, we'll compare some of the different songs and the colors they brought to mind. We'll see if we can identify the elements of those songs that remind us of colors.

(continued)

WHAT COLOR IS THIS SONG?

(continued)

FOLLOW-UP

Assign students to work in small groups. (See Chapter Three for quick and easy ways to randomly assign student work teams.) Repeat the activity (with different music) and ask each group to come up with at least one color for each song, along with a reason for choosing that color.

VARIATION

Instead of using paper and pencils, invite students to write their color choices on a large dry-erase or whiteboard while the music is playing. Each student can choose more than one color for each song. After the music stops, discuss the contributions posted. (If you don't have a whiteboard, use a large sheet of butcher paper for each song.)

119. SONG SWITCH

⭐ **PURPOSE:** music icebreaker ⭐ **AGES:** 7–adult

⭐ **TIME:** 10–20 minutes

⭐ **MATERIALS:** selection of familiar songs, index cards, paper and pens or pencils

PREPARATION

Create a selection of songs that will be familiar to your students, given their age, culture, and geographical location ("Jingle Bells," "Jailhouse Rock," "911 Is a Joke," "God Blessed Texas," "I Wanna Hold Your Hand," or current pop songs). Write the name of each song on each of two different index cards to create a matching pair.

Type or copy the lyrics to a few verses or the chorus of each song. Make copies of the lyrics to hand out to students after they have formed their teams.

Greet students as they arrive and give each student an index card, a few sheets of paper, and a pen or pencil.

INSTRUCTIONS FOR STUDENTS

1 Before we begin our musical activity, your first task is to locate your partner by finding the person who has the same song title on his or her index card. You have __ seconds (or minutes) to locate your partners. Go. *[Use your Attention Getter to signal that the time is up and you need everyone's quiet attention for the next instruction. See the Introduction for details on creating effective Attention Getters.]*

2 Your mission is to rewrite the lyrics of at least one verse of your song. You will have __ minutes to do this. I will be coming around to give each team the original lyrics for their songs. I will give you a one-minute warning when the time is almost up.

Note: If you have students who have recently moved to your country, make sure they are assigned to work with local partners who can help them with any unfamiliar songs.

FOLLOW-UP

Invite each team to present its revised lyrics to the class. See if classmates can identify the original song.

VARIATIONS

Instead of rewriting lyrics, have students revise the songs by changing the rhythm or beat of a song (from pop to classical, for example).

If you have a computer available, allow students to type out their lyrics.

Chapter Fourteen

Swell Ideas for ELLs

One of the most enjoyable aspects of teaching English language learners (ELLs)—which includes teaching English as a second language (ESL)—is that students who voluntarily enroll in those classes tend to be highly motivated and cooperative—they love learning.

They do their homework. In fact, they often request more homework so they can learn faster. In other cases, where students are assigned to an ESL class because of poor academic performance or test scores, they may be more reluctant to learn. But overall it has been my experience that if you provide material and information that are personally relevant to ELL students' lives, they will be quickly engaged.

Designing icebreakers for beginning-level ELLs can be a challenge, because students may not understand even simple verbal instructions. That's why the instructions in these activities are presented in a different format from those in the previous chapters. Instructions here are presented as a series of steps, not as spoken instructions for students. Teachers can decide, depending on their individual classes, when verbal instructions are appropriate and when gestures or modeling would be more helpful to students.

120. BODY PARTS

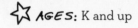 **PURPOSE:** English language learners icebreaker   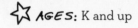 **AGES:** K and up

 TIME: 10–20 minutes

 MATERIALS: card stock, bold marker, photos or drawings of body parts

PREPARATION

On card stock draw or paste large pictures of various body parts. Label each body part appropriately (in the singular or the plural—eye or *eyes*, for example). On the back of each card, print just the label without a picture.

Step 1. Choose a card with a picture or label. Hold up the card and say the body part. As you say the body part, touch that part of your own body. Repeat the word and cue students to touch that part of their own bodies.

Choose another card and repeat the same process: say the word, touch the body part, cue the students. Continue until you have gone through 5 cards a few times. (Our working memories can hold only 5–9 bits of new information, so try to avoid using too many new cards at one time.)

Step 2. Repeat the activity using only the backs of the same 5 cards, so students see just the labels without pictures. Hold up a card, say the word, and see how many students can locate the correct body part.

Repeat the same 5 body parts again, this time just speaking the words, without showing any cards.

Step 3. Introduce 5 new cards and body parts, and repeat Steps 1 and 2.

Step 4. Touch three body parts in sequence, saying each part as you touch it: for example *eyes, ears, nose;* or *knees, waist, shoulders.* Cue students to mimic your motions and words. After they have the idea, say the words without touching your own body, to make the exercise more challenging.

Increase the challenge further by adding two-handed touches: both hands on *knees knees, ears ears, hair.*

Step 5. Add verbs such as *wiggle, wave, lift, stomp,* and *open* to your cues. Wiggle your fingers. Wave your arms. Lift your right foot. Stomp your left foot. Open your mouth.

(continued)

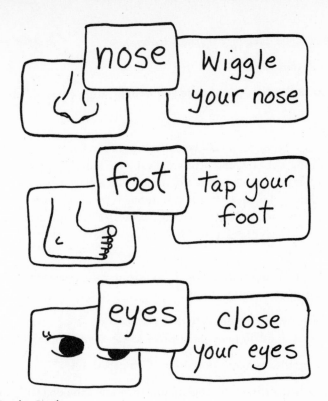

Sample Body Parts Poster

121. LET'S TALK

☆ **PURPOSE**: English language learners icebreaker

☆ **AGES**: 6-adult

☆ **TIME**: 10-20 minutes

☆ **MATERIALS**: butcher paper or poster board

PREPARATION

Create a series of age-appropriate conversations between two speakers, using the social and cultural activities, hobbies, and academic subjects that engage your students.

Print each conversation on a poster board or a piece of butcher paper in letters large enough to be read from the back of your classroom. Give each conversation a unique label, such as After School, At Lunch, Playing Soccer, Visiting the Zoo, or At the Movies.

Write the name of each conversation on two separate slips of paper. Save these to use when assigning partners.

Step 1. Choose one conversation. Read the title and the conversation aloud to help students learn proper pronunciation.

Step 2. Ask for student volunteers to take turns acting as the speakers and reading the conversations aloud. Repeat each conversation several times.

Step 3. Select another conversation. Repeat Steps 1 and 2.

Step 4. Randomly distribute the slips of paper bearing the conversation titles. Give students one minute to match up their slips and locate their partners. (If you have an uneven number of students, the teacher or aide should participate in the practice.)

Step 5. Partners practice saying the conversations together for 5-10 minutes. Then collect the slips of paper, redistribute them to form new partnerships, and continue practicing.

VARIATIONS

Instead of writing the conversations out on butcher paper, write them on slides and project them onto a screen or wall where they are clearly visible to everybody.

Type conversations, print them, and distribute them to students to practice in pairs.

Create longer conversations for more advanced students. Or ask them to work in pairs and write out their own conversations. Type and make copies of the conversations and exchange them among pairs for practice.

LET'S TALK

122. NOSES TO TOES

⭐ **PURPOSE:** English language learners icebreaker   ⭐ **AGES:** 7–adult

⭐ **TIME:** 10–20 minutes

⭐ **MATERIALS:** labeled and unlabeled posters showing human body parts

PREPARATION

Create a template with the outline of a human figure with body parts labeled. Find a sample online at *http://eastsideliteracy.org/tutorsupport/documents/HO_Body.pdf*.

If you can't access the online poster, draw the outline of a figure and label the following parts: head, eye, ear, mouth, nose, neck, chin, shoulder, chest, arm, elbow, belly button, waist, wrist, hand, finger, hip, thigh, leg, knee, shin, heel, ankle, foot, and toe.

Create a blank template of the same poster without labels. You can find a blank poster at *http://eastsideliteracy.org/tutorsupport/documents/HO_UnBody.pdf*.

Make copies of the labeled posters and the blank posters for students. If possible, create a large labeled poster to display in the classroom, or create a slide and project the poster on a screen or wall where it is clearly visible to all students. Make sure labels are printed large enough for students in the back of the room to read them easily.

Step 1. Distribute the labeled posters first. Read each label out loud and cue students to repeat each label as you read it. Cue them to touch the body part as they say its name. (By adding movement, you enhance long-term memory storage.)

Step 2. Choose a random body part. Say its name. Ask students to point to it on their posters and repeat the name.

Step 3. Ask students to turn the posters facedown on their desks and stand up. Say a body part. Cue them to touch that body part on their own bodies.

Step 4. Collect the labeled posters. Remove your labeled poster from display or turn off the projector so the labels are no longer visible.

Step 5. Assign students to work in pairs. Give each pair an unlabeled poster. See how many labels they can correctly fill in.

FOLLOW-UP

Repeat Step 5 the following day and again later in the week as a review.

VARIATION

For younger students, limit the number of body parts on the chart to avoid causing frustration. Start with 5–10 and add more labels each day until the chart is completely labeled.

Taken from *Kick-Start Your Class: Academic Icebreakers to Engage Students.* Copyright © 2012 by LouAnne Johnson. Reproduced by permission of Jossey-Bass, an Imprint of Wiley. www.josseybass.com.

123. SCHOOL SHOPPERS

☆ **PURPOSE:** English language learners icebreaker   ☆ **AGES:** 7–adult

☆ **TIME:** 10–20 minutes

☆ **MATERIALS:** binders, spiral notebooks, pencils, pens, rules, staplers, paper clips, paper, highlighters

PREPARATION

Place your school supplies in various locations around the classroom. Create a number of different shopping lists that include different amounts of numbers of various supplies. For example, one list might include

> 2 spiral notebooks
>
> 5 sheets of lined paper
>
> 3 sheets of blank paper
>
> 1 stapler
>
> 15 paper clips
>
> 1 yellow highlighter

Another list might read

> 2 blue highlighters
>
> 1 stapler
>
> 2 boxes of staples
>
> 4 yellow paper clips
>
> 1 binder

Make several copies of each list.
Optional: Provide paper or plastic shopping bags.

Step 1. Give each student a shopping list (and a bag, if you have them). Give them 3 minutes to collect the items on their lists from around the classroom.

Step 2. Check each shopping list against the items collected. Discuss any questions about colors, numbers, or names of items.

(continued)

SCHOOL SHOPPERS

(continued)

Step 3. Have students return the supplies to their original locations. Give them a time limit to increase motivation and engagement.

Step 4. Exchange shopping lists and repeat the activity.

VARIATIONS

Instead of actual school supplies, provide pictures of supplies for students to collect on their shopping trips. Make multiple copies of pictures so students can collect the items they need and assemble them on a desk where the teacher can check their list against the pictures.

Provide pencils and paper. Provide a scenario such as going to the beach, taking a vacation, watching a baseball game, going on a picnic, or visiting grandparents. Ask students to make a list of items they might bring for each different activity. Invite volunteers to share their lists with the class.

Special note: Consider asking local business owners to donate reusable shopping bags or school supplies for students to keep. Offer to write a letter to the editor of the local newspaper thanking the business(es) for their generosity. Have students write thank-you letters and send the letters along with a class photo to any participating businesses. Many businesses appreciate the opportunity to contribute to schools—they enjoy giving, and it's excellent advertising along with a tax deduction for them.

124. PICTURE PAIRS

☆ **PURPOSE**: English language learners icebreaker   ☆ **AGES**: 5–adult

☆ **TIME**: 10–20 minutes

☆ **MATERIALS**: card stock, bold markers, pictures

PREPARATION

Find or draw a set of 10–20 pictures of people, places, animals, and objects. Make copies of the picture set on card stock so you have one set for each student in class.

In large letters, print the name of each picture on a separate card.

Step 1. Distribute picture card sets to students.

Step 2. Hold up each name card one at a time. Read the name aloud. Hold up the matching picture card. Cue students to repeat the name and hold up their matching picture cards. Repeat this activity two or three times, if appropriate, for practice.

Step 3. Randomly select a name card from the set. Hold it up and say the name aloud. Cue students to say the name and hold up the matching picture card.

Step 4. Repeat the activity, without showing the name card. Say the name of each picture, and cue students to repeat the name and hold up the appropriate picture card.

Step 5. This time around, hold up a word card but do not say the word aloud. Students say the word and hold up the matching picture card.

Step 6. For the final go-round, do not display the word cards. Simply pronounce a word and ask students to hold up the correct picture card.

FOLLOW-UP

Create a concentration-style game using one word card for each picture card in a desk. Turn all the cards face down. Students take turns turning two cards faceup to see if they can locate the picture card to match each word card. If their two cards match, they remove them from the table. If they don't match, they are turned facedown and the next player takes a turn. The game ends when all cards are matched.

VARIATIONS

Reverse the process by providing students with sets of name cards. When the teacher displays a picture, students hold up the matching name card and say the word aloud in unison.

For adults or advanced learners, use phrases and complex pictures of activities and scenes such as hiking in the mountains, shopping for shoes, attending a wedding, or ordering a meal instead of single words and simple pictures.

Taken from *Kick-Start Your Class: Academic Icebreakers to Engage Students.* Copyright © 2012 by LouAnne Johnson. Reproduced by permission of Jossey-Bass, an Imprint of Wiley. www.josseybass.com.

125. TAKE A NOTE

☆ **PURPOSE:** English language learners icebreaker   ☆ **AGES:** 7–adult

☆ **TIME:** 10–20 minutes

☆ **MATERIALS:** writing paper; pencils or pens; or whiteboards and dry-erase markers

PREPARATION

Write out a set of five or ten sentences, using vocabulary that is appropriate for the age and ability of your students. For beginners, use short simple sentences. For intermediate or advanced students, add a few compound and complex sentences and include some sentences with varied punctuation, such as quotation marks, apostrophes, and question marks.

Step 1. One at a time, dictate sentences to students. Have them write each sentence down on paper. *(Be prepared for reluctance, as many English language learners hesitate to write imperfect sentences. Assure them that you will work together to correct any spelling or grammar errors. Their job is to get the sentences down on paper so they can see them. Explain that they earn full credit for writing the sentences, regardless of errors.)*

Step 2. After all the sentences have been dictated and written, ask for volunteers to go to the board and write each sentence.

Step 3. Discuss each sentence as a whole class and have the student volunteer make any necessary corrections as directed by students. When the class is satisfied that they have corrected the sentence, the teacher verifies the corrections or asks for further modifications until the sentence is correct.

Step 4. Have students turn their papers over. Erase the board and dictate the same sentences. Ask for volunteers to write the sentences again. Discuss and correct each sentence.

VARIATION

Ask students to create their own sentences to dictate to the group. Ask volunteers to write sentences on the board. Discuss each sentence as a class, making any necessary corrections.

Special note: We used this exercise with great success when I taught ESL adults at a community college in North Carolina. Many of the students had been in the United States for a number of years and could speak English well, but could not write a simple sentence. They resisted writing because they couldn't do it perfectly. We worked on becoming comfortable with making mistakes. After a year of dictation, many of those students gained enough confidence and skills to move up to GED-level classes.

TAKE A NOTE

PART THREE
Forty Ways to Wrap It Up

Endings can be as important as beginnings when it comes to learning. Although it may be tempting to skip the closure activities in view of time constraints, even a brief refresher can make a big difference for learners. When we reframe, reinforce, and revisit new learning, student retention of that new learning improves.

Why Closure Counts

Closure is not the same as simply reviewing new material. Generally, during review sessions the teacher does most of the talking and most of the mental work—checking for student understanding of key concepts or skills from recent lessons. During closure activities, teachers don't give answers—they ask questions. They guide students by providing opportunities for students to consider new information or ideas and practice newly acquired skills.

Whether students are using rote rehearsal methods (repeating the multiplication tables or the alphabet) or more elaborate rehearsal (forming their own conclusions about new information or demonstrating new skills), the point is to provide an opportunity for students to interact with content personally and individually. The saying "Use it or lose it" really applies in this case. Without rehearsal, long-term retention of information and skills simply doesn't happen.

It Is Brain Science!

"Don't let your students leave class without doing a closure activity—it's bad science and poor teaching." That advice comes from brain researchers and teachers Eric Jensen and LeAnn Nickelsen in their excellent book, *Deeper Learning: 7 Powerful Strategies for In-Depth and Longer-Lasting Learning* (Corwin Press, 2008). The authors explain that closure is a "big-picture processing activity" that enables students to assemble and connect the various chunks of information they have learned during a lesson. This book includes a number of quick closure activities that allow the teacher to gauge the understanding of every student. The Door Pass, for example, requires each student to write down a question or statement that meets criteria set by the teacher in order to be allowed to leave the room. Although the authors provide sample questions for older students, the length and complexity of the criteria for the door pass can easily be altered to suit the age and ability of younger students. You could opt to use a verbal door pass instead of a written one, for example.

This part of the book has a slightly different format from the previous two parts. Instead of instructions for students, you will find preparation guidelines and steps for implementing each activity, without specific instructions, since closure activities nearly always need to be modified to suit a particular academic environment and student population. Chapter Fifteen offers twenty suggestions for daily closure that also can be used periodically during a given class to reinforce new learning before making the transition to a new or related topic. Chapter Sixteen focuses on end-of-term activities that help students process what they have learned and arrive at a sense of completion.

As always, please tweak these activities to suit yourself and your students— then pass them on to your colleagues. If you create an activity that works wonderfully well, consider posting it on one of the many online websites for teachers. New teachers especially need and appreciate effective teaching strategies.

Chapter Fifteen

What We Learned Today: Daily Closure

*D*aily closure activities can be used to summarize and emphasize essential elements of a lesson.

They can also be used to encourage students to reflect and think about new material, connect new information to previous knowledge, relate one subject area to another, reframe new skills and concepts—*How else can I use what I have just learned?*—and predict what comes next on the agenda.

Closure activities don't have to be as elaborate as the ones suggested in this chapter. They can be as simple as providing one or two minutes for students to write in their learning logs or think about what they have learned before responding to a question. The more complex the concepts in a lesson, the more rehearsal students will need. The format of your closure exercises isn't important, as long as they achieve the purpose: giving your students' brains the best possible opportunity to process new information and skills.

1. ABCs

⭐ **CATEGORY:** daily or single lesson closure activity   ⭐ **AGES:** 7 and up

⭐ **TIME:** 5-15 minutes

⭐ **MATERIALS:** whiteboard and markers or chalkboard and chalk

⭐ **PURPOSE:** reinforce new skill(s) or information, address student questions and concerns, connect new material to previous learning, create personal meaning to improve student retention of new information and/or skills

PROCEDURE

Step 1. Write A, B, and C in large letters across the board to create three vertical columns. Below the letter A print:

An important fact, lesson, or skill we learned today.

Below the letter B write:

Big questions about what we learned today.

And under the letter C write:

Connection to something else we already know or can do.

Step 2. First, invite students to offer examples for column A. Write all student input under column A before proceeding.

Step 3. Addressing each topic in column A one at a time, invite student input for columns B and C. There may be multiple suggestions for columns B and C.

Step 4. Thank the students for thinking and participating.

VARIATIONS

To add a kinesthetic element, students can go to the board and write their own ideas under each column.

With older students, a volunteer may be asked to lead the discussion on each topic, or students may complete their own ABC worksheets and share them with partners, teams, or the whole class.

Adult students may work in teams to create bullet points on butcher paper or easels to present to the class.

2. BALL TOSS RECAP

⭐ **CATEGORY:** daily or single lesson closure activity   ⭐ **AGES:** 6 and up

⭐ **TIME:** 5-15 minutes

⭐ **MATERIALS:** soft rubber or cloth ball

⭐ **PURPOSE:** reinforce and review new information, create personal meaning to improve student retention of recently acquired information

PROCEDURE

Step 1. Begin by asking a question about the lesson just completed. Toss the ball to a student, who must answer the question.

Step 2. If the student's answer is incorrect, the student tosses the ball to another student, who attempts to answer. This continues until somebody correctly answers the question.

Step 3. When a student correctly answers a question, that student then poses the next question and tosses the ball to a classmate who must answer. Repeat Steps 2 and 3.

VARIATIONS

Instead of posing questions, you can give students the option of making a statement about something important they learned during the lesson and then tossing the ball to a classmate.

Assign students to small groups and let them play the ball toss among their team. This will allow more participation from each student. You can roam around to provide encouragement and verify correct answers when there is doubt.

Variation for physical education, music, or dance teachers: toss the ball to a student who must then perform a specific new skill from the day's lesson. The student then tosses the ball to a classmate who must perform the same skill or a different one.

3. BIG BANNER

☆ *CATEGORY*: daily or single lesson closure activity   ☆ *AGES*: 7 and up

☆ *TIME*: 5–15 minutes

☆ *MATERIALS*: roll of butcher paper, markers

☆ *PURPOSE*: reinforce and review information, create personal meaning to improve student retention of new information and/or skill(s)

PROCEDURE

Step 1. Post a large sheet of butcher paper on a wall and provide students with markers. For a large class, post two or more sheets of paper.

Step 2. Invite students to come up at their discretion and write on the paper the important things they remember learning in the recently completed lesson or during the day. Multiple comments on the same topic are fine; student comments don't need to be original or unique.

Step 3. Circle key concepts or important lesson elements and invite future student comments on those topics.

Step 4. Completed lists can be posted on the wall or stored for future reference. They can be used to review for a quiz or exam.

Step 5 (optional). At the end of a unit or course, hang all of the banners around the room as a visible representation of the learning that has taken place. This creates an impressive motivational visual for students.

(continued)

BIG BANNER

208

(continued)

VARIATIONS

If students have individual whiteboards, ask them to create their lists on their own or working in pairs.

Skills-based lessons: If students have recently learned a new skill rather than new information, ask for volunteers to demonstrate. Or assign students to work in pairs and demonstrate the skill for each other. The teacher participates only if a question arises. Otherwise students teach and critique each other's performance. (Students may need coaching or demonstrations of how to perform helpful peer critiques.)

BIG BANNER

4. BOARD BINGO

☆ *CATEGORY:* daily or single lesson closure activity   ☆ *AGES:* 6 and up

☆ *TIME:* 10–20 minutes

☆ *MATERIALS:* dry-erase board, whiteboard, chalkboard, or paper and markers

☆ *PURPOSE:* review and reinforce new learning, create personal meaning to improve student retention of recently acquired information

PROCEDURE

Step 1. Using dry-erase markers or chalk, create a large 9-square bingo template on the whiteboard or chalkboard where it is easily visible to all students.

Step 2. Fill in six random squares with key concept from the recently completed lesson. This can be done by you alone or with input from students. Leave three squares blank.

Step 3. Students copy the bingo template onto sheets of paper for personal use. Each student fills in the three blank spaces with key concepts printed in the six completed squares so that student cards are different from each other. (You may opt to allow students one "FREE" space where they can place a marker for any one question.)

While students are copying the template, copy each key concept onto a slip of paper and place the slips into a bag.

Step 4. Distribute pennies, poker chips, or beans for students to use as markers.

Step 5. Draw one slip at a time from the bag and read out the concept. Students place a marker over the corresponding square on their papers.

Step 6. The first student to complete three in a row or all four corners is the winner. Students clear their cards, and the winner draws slips for the second game.

VARIATION

If time or student ability is an issue, the teacher can create the template and make copies to distribute to students. To quickly prepare for this activity, teachers can create a blank template and make copies to use as needed.

5. CARTOON QUOTES

☆ **CATEGORY:** daily or single lesson closure activity   ☆ **AGES:** 6 and up

☆ **TIME:** 5-15 minutes

☆ **MATERIALS:** dry-erase board, whiteboard, chalkboard, or poster board

☆ **PURPOSE:** review and reinforce new learning, address student questions and/or concerns about new learning, create personal meaning to improve student retention of recently acquired information

PROCEDURE

Step 1. On the board, draw large cartoon characters with big blank dialogue bubbles.

Step 2. Ask students to fill in the bubbles so the characters are discussing information from the most recent lesson(s) the students have studied. Students can give input for you to write down or they can fill in the bubbles themselves.

Step 3. Discuss the completed dialogue and address any questions or concerns.

Step 4. Erase the dialogue and fill in the bubbles with new words. Discuss.

VARIATIONS

Create a poster, laminate it, and use an erasable marker so the poster can be reused as desired. Or create a blank template and make copies for students to fill in on their own.

Assign students to work in pairs or groups. Give teams a few minutes to come up with suggestions to fill in the dialogue bubbles. Take turns filling them in and discuss each completed conversation.

6 CONNECT THE DOTS

☆ **CATEGORY:** daily or single lesson closure activity   ☆ **AGES:** 7 and up

☆ **TIME:** 5–15 minutes

☆ **MATERIALS:** dry-erase board, whiteboard, chalkboard, or paper and pens or pencils

☆ **PURPOSE:** reinforce new skill(s) or information, address student questions and concerns, connect new material to previous learning, create personal meaning to improve student retention of new information and/or skills

PROCEDURE

Step 1. Draw a large dot on the board and write the name of a key concept students recently learned or studied.

Step 2. Invite students to come to the board and create their own dots, adding something they learned about the concept at the main dot, something they already knew about the concept, or something they learned in another class that is related or connected to this concept.

Step 3. The student draws a line from the new dot to the main dot or to other dots that are related or connected in some way.

Step 4. As each student adds a dot, you and the class discuss the addition.

VARIATION

Provide paper and pencils or pens and ask students to create their own dot connections. After students finish, ask them to share their dots with the class or with a partner or team. Roam around the room, providing assistance or clarification where needed.

7. COUNTDOWN: 3, 2, 1

☆ **CATEGORY:** daily or single lesson closure activity   ☆ **AGES:** 6 and up

☆ **TIME:** 5–15 minutes

☆ **MATERIALS:** dry-erase board, whiteboard, chalkboard, markers or chalk

☆ **PURPOSE:** reinforce new skill(s) or information, address student questions and concerns, connect new material to previous learning, create personal meaning to improve student retention of new information and/or skills

PROCEDURE

Step 1. On the left side of the board, write large numbers 3, 2, and 1 in a vertical column.

Step 2. Invite students to share three things they learned that day. Write each new item to the right of the numeral 3.

Step 3. Invite students to share two things they learned the previous day (or week). Write these new items to the right of numeral 2.

Step 4. Invite students to suggest one thing they predict they might learn the next day or the next week. Write this item to the right of numeral 1.

Step 5. If time permits, erase the items and repeat the exercise with new suggestions from students.

VARIATIONS

Instead of completing this activity on the board, students write 3, 2, 1 on their papers and fill in the information themselves. Then ask for volunteers to share what they wrote and have the class discuss the students' input.

For younger students, this entire exercise can be completed verbally with just the 3, 2, 1 numbers on the board for reference.

8. FLASH CARDS

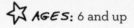

☆ **CATEGORY:** daily or single lesson closure activity

☆ **AGES:** 6 and up

☆ **TIME:** 10-20 minutes

☆ **MATERIALS:** index cards or poster board

☆ **PURPOSE:** reinforce new skill(s) or information, address student questions and concerns, connect new material to previous learning, create personal meaning to improve student retention of new information and/or skills

PROCEDURE

Step 1. Create several cards that include facts, questions, and pictures or illustrations to represent key concepts or skills recently learned or acquired by students. If appropriate, answers or clues can be added to the backs of cards.

Step 2. Working in pairs or small groups, each team of students receives 4-5 cards to discuss and interpret within a specific time period.

Step 3. At the end of the time period, students exchange cards and discuss the new set.

Step 4. Move around the room, providing guidance and clarification as needed.

VARIATIONS

Instead of smaller cards to be used by individual students, you can create large poster-sized cards to be used by the whole class.

Students can create their own flash card sets to use as study aids. They can trade their card sets to foster student bonding and encourage discussions about learning.

9. FRACTURED PHRASES

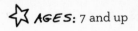

☆ **CATEGORY:** daily or single lesson closure activity

☆ **AGES:** 7 and up

☆ **TIME:** 5-15 minutes

☆ **MATERIALS:** projector and screen

☆ **PURPOSE:** reinforce new skill(s) or information, address student questions and concerns, create personal meaning to improve student retention of new information and/or skills

PROCEDURE

Step 1. Create a series of slides featuring phrases or sentences about a recent lesson—but jumble the words so they are not in the correct sequence. For example:

> of Declaration the Independence
>
> triangle equilateral has an 3 sides equal
>
> population Brazil million the of 200 approximately is

Step 2. Project one slide at a time. Students try to rearrange the words to make a logical phrase or sentence as quickly as they can.

Step 3. Lead a quick discussion of each phrase or sentence, addressing student questions or concerns about the information or skill involved.

VARIATIONS

This exercise can be modified to include diagrams, illustrations, math problems, or other information pertinent to a specific lesson or subject. For language arts students, slides can include sentences that have grammatical or spelling errors needing correction, or you can ask students to identify prepositions, adverbs, and so on.

If no projector or screen is available, this exercise can be completed using a whiteboard and dry-erase markers, with the teacher writing each phrase and erasing it after students have corrected and discussed it.

10. LEARNING TREE OR GARDEN

⭐ **CATEGORY:** daily or single lesson closure activity

⭐ **AGES:** 6 and up

⭐ **TIME:** 5–10 minutes

⭐ **MATERIALS:** construction paper, scissors, markers

⭐ **PURPOSE:** reinforce new skill(s) or information, address student questions and concerns, create personal meaning to improve student retention of new information and/or skills

PROCEDURE

Step 1. Using green and brown construction paper, create a tree with many branches or a row of plants with multiple stems rising upward.

Step 2. Cut out multiple leaves and blossoms from various colors of construction paper.

Step 3. At the end of a lesson, invite students to write on the leaves and blossoms something they have learned about a specific topic, skill, or concept. (You may need to write down the responses from younger students and beginning writers.)

Step 4. Students tape or tack their leaves and blossoms to the tree or plants to create a visual representation of their new learning.

VARIATION

Install a real or artificial tree in one corner of the classroom. As new information or skills are learned, add blossoms to the tree using pipe cleaners or other nonharmful items.

LEARNING TREE OR GARDEN

11. LITTLE WHITEBOARD REVIEW

☆ *CATEGORY*: daily or single lesson closure activity   ☆ *AGES*: 7 and up

☆ *TIME*: 5-10 minutes

☆ *MATERIALS*: individual dry-erase or whiteboards and dry-erase markers, projector (optional)

☆ *PURPOSE*: reinforce new skill(s) or information, address student questions and concerns, create personal meaning to improve student retention of new information and/or skills

PROCEDURE

Step 1. Create a series of questions that require short answers or multiple-choice answers (generally, short answers allow you to assess student learning more accurately than a multiple-choice format, since they do not provide any prompting).

Step 2. Ask one question at a time and have students respond by writing the answer to each question on their whiteboards. (If possible, project each question on a screen to aid visual learners or those who do not easily process auditory input.)

Step 3. Either on cue or as soon as they are finished, students hold up their whiteboards for you to view.

Step 4. Quickly nod or point at each board with a *Yes* or a *No*. Students who receive a *No* can try again or ask a classmate for help.

Step 5. Address any student concerns or confusion about the topic before moving on to the next question.

Step 6. As this activity continues, keep a tally mark on a copy of your roster to indicate students who may need follow-up review on a particular topic.

VARIATION

Invite students to create questions for the class to answer on their whiteboards.

12. MISSING WORDS

⭐ **CATEGORY:** daily or single lesson closure activity   ⭐ **AGES:** 7 and up

⭐ **TIME:** 5–15 minutes

⭐ **MATERIALS:** dry-erase board, whiteboard or chalkboard and markers or chalk, or projector

⭐ **PURPOSE:** reinforce new skill(s) or information, address student questions and concerns, connect new learning to previous learning, create personal meaning to improve student retention of new information and/or skills

PROCEDURE

Step 1. Write a sentence on the board about the day's lesson topic with one or more key words missing from the sentence. (If a projector is available, you can project sentences onto a screen or wall, and students can either write down the missing words or respond verbally.)

Step 2. Students fill in the missing word, either by writing it on paper or a whiteboard, or by responding verbally.

Step 3. Lead a quick discussion after each sentence, checking for student understanding and correcting any student misconceptions.

VARIATIONS

If time permits, you can make up the sentences ahead of time, type them out, and print copies for each student to complete individually. Students who need more time can opt to take the handout home to complete it and return it the following day (or next class meeting).

You can assign students to work in pairs or groups to create their own sentences with missing words for classmates to fill in.

13. PAIR SHARES

⭐ **CATEGORY:** daily or single lesson closure activity   ⭐ **AGES:** 6 and up

⭐ **TIME:** 5-15 minutes

⭐ **MATERIALS:** none required

⭐ **PURPOSE:** reinforce new skill(s) or information, address student questions and concerns, connect new learning to previous learning, create personal meaning to improve student retention of new information and/or skills

PROCEDURE

Step 1. Assign students to work in pairs. If there is an uneven number of students in the class, you or an aide can participate, or you can form one student trio. It's best to count students beforehand to be prepared and to avoid making any students feel "left out" when partners are assigned. (See Chapter Three for quick and easy methods of randomly assigning partners.)

Step 2. Designate one student to begin as speaker and the other as listener at the start of the activity.

Step 3. On cue, students have a predetermined amount of time (such as 30 seconds, 1 minute, or 5 minutes) to share with each other what they remember from the day's lesson(s). Limiting the amount of time adds a sense of urgency to the activity.

Step 4. Give students a signal halfway through the time period, so they can switch roles from speaker to listener.

Step 5. If time permits, ask each pair to quickly summarize their conversation for the class. Or students can create bullet points listing key concepts or facts on a sheet of paper to share with the class.

VARIATIONS

This activity can be used several times during any lesson to promote student engagement and understanding.

You can adapt this activity to include connections to previous learning by posing questions that refer to past lessons for pair-share conversations.

14. PAPER AIRPLANES

☆ *CATEGORY*: daily or single lesson closure activity   ☆ *AGES*: 7 and up

☆ *TIME*: 10–20 minutes

☆ *MATERIALS*: scrap paper or recycled paper, pens or pencils

☆ *PURPOSE*: reinforce new skill(s) or information, address student questions and concerns, create personal meaning to improve student retention of new information and/or skills

PROCEDURE

Step 1. Provide each student with one or more pieces of paper.

Step 2. Students write a question about the current topic of study and fold the paper into a paper airplane. Students sail their airplanes into the air (in an upward direction and not at each other).

Step 3. Each student then picks up an airplane, reads the question, and formulates an answer. The student can refer to reference material as needed to formulate an answer.

Step 4. Select students at random to read their questions and present their answers. Classmates offers suggestions as needed to improve the answers.

VARIATION

Instead of paper airplanes, have students squash their papers into ball shapes and toss them across the room. Again, students may need to be instructed to toss their balls onto desktops or the floor and not at classmates.

PAPER AIRPLANES

15. QUESTION OF THE DAY

⭐ **CATEGORY:** daily or single lesson closure activity   ⭐ **AGES:** 7 and up

⭐ **TIME:** 5–15 minutes

⭐ **MATERIALS:** slips of paper, pens or pencils, a bag or box

⭐ **PURPOSE:** reinforce new skill(s) or information, address student questions and concerns, create personal meaning to improve student retention of new information and/or skills

PROCEDURE

Step 1. Provide each student with one or more slips of paper.

Step 2. Students write down one question about the current lesson on each slip of paper.

Step 3. Collect all the questions in a box or bag.

Step 4. A student volunteer draws out a single question for whole-class, small-group, or pair-share discussions.

Step 5. If time permits, student volunteers take turns drawing out several questions for quick answers and brief discussions.

VARIATION

You can connect new learning to previous learning by adding questions to the box that refer to past lessons.

16. QUIZ QUESTIONS

☆ **CATEGORY:** daily or single lesson closure activity   ☆ **AGES:** 7 and up

☆ **TIME:** 5–15 minutes

☆ **MATERIALS:** paper, bag or box

☆ **PURPOSE:** reinforce new skill(s) or information, address student questions and concerns, create personal meaning to improve student retention of new information and/or skills

PROCEDURE

Step 1. Provide each student with one slip of paper.

Step 2. Students create one quiz-style question about the lesson.

Step 3. Collect all the questions and place them in a box or bag.

Step 4. Draw out questions one at a time to create an impromptu quiz.

VARIATIONS

Instead of holding an impromptu quiz, review the questions and use them to create an oral or written quiz for the following day.

To foster thinking, you can read out the students' quiz questions without discussing the answers. The following day you can review the questions and ask for student responses.

17. RATE THE LESSON

⭐ **CATEGORY:** daily or single lesson closure activity   ⭐ **AGES:** 7 and up

⭐ **TIME:** 5-15 minutes

⭐ **MATERIALS:** index cards, pens or pencils, poster board

⭐ **PURPOSE:** reinforce new skill(s) or information, address student questions and concerns, create personal meaning to improve student retention of new information and/or skills

PROCEDURE

Step 1. At the end of a lesson, draw a simple scale on the board, using the numbers 1-5 and the following labels (or something along these lines):

1. *Excellent.* I understand or I can do this on my own.

2. *Good.* I just need a little more practice or study.

3. *Okay.* I'm getting it, but I still have a few questions.

4. *Not very good.* It was too hard or too easy for me.

5. *Terrible.* I am completely lost and frustrated.

Step 2. Distribute index cards to students.

Step 3. Each student writes his or her name and a number from 1-5 to rate the lesson. Students also write at least one sentence to explain their rating.

Step 4. Take a quick tally by asking students for a thumbs-up for each number on the scale. A secret vote can be taken by having students hold their fists against their chests as they vote, so their thumb is not visible to others.

Step 5. Collect the cards and review them to see if further study, demonstration, or review is needed before moving on to the next lesson.

VARIATIONS

If a computer is available, you can create a slide of the rating scale that can be projected whenever students are asked to rate a lesson.

With younger students, you might choose to skip the written comments and ask students to respond verbally or rate the lesson by holding up their fingers to indicate their chosen ratings.

18. ROGER RECAP

☆ **CATEGORY:** daily or single lesson closure activity    **AGES:** 5 and up

☆ **TIME:** 5–15 minutes

☆ **MATERIALS:** stuffed animal or hand puppet

☆ **PURPOSE:** reinforce new skill(s) or information, address student questions and concerns, create personal meaning to improve student retention of new information and/or skills

PROCEDURE

Step 1. At the end of a lesson, introduce a stuffed animal or puppet named Roger Recap (or an appropriate name for the age of students). Roger is very smart, but sometimes he forgets things. He needs help.

Step 2. Roger asks questions (or whispers them into your ear) about the lesson. Then you ask for volunteers to answer Roger's questions.

Step 3. Ask students for advice on what Roger should do at home to practice or understand the lesson better.

VARIATION

If it suits your personality, you can do this activity with older students who have been taught and encouraged to participate in role-play and similar activities. Sometimes teachers assume that older students will think an activity is "too silly" to do, but older students often enjoy such activities as good ways to relieve stress and tension, in addition to reinforcing new learning.

19. SENTENCE STARTERS

☆ **CATEGORY:** daily or single lesson closure activity   ☆ **AGES:** 6 and up

☆ **TIME:** 5–15 minutes

☆ **MATERIALS:** index cards, paper and pens or pencils

☆ **PURPOSE:** reinforce new skill(s) or information, address student questions and concerns, create personal meaning to improve student retention of new information and/or skills

PROCEDURE

Step 1. At the end of a lesson, write one or more unfinished sentences on the board. For example:

> Today I learned . . .
>
> I have a question about . . .
>
> I wonder . . .
>
> I'm still confused about . . .
>
> I think . . .

Step 2. Distribute index cards or sheets of paper to students.

Step 3. Students finish the sentence(s).

Step 4. Collect the finished sentences and quickly review them before holding a quick class discussion to correct misunderstandings or answer questions. Or, instead of collecting the finished sentences, ask for volunteers to share their completed sentences. Student responses may spark discussions.

VARIATIONS

Instead of collecting or discussing the sentences as initially described, you can treat them as Exit Tickets that students must hand in before they can leave the room. You then review the sentences to see whether the class is ready to move on and which students may need some additional coaching or instruction.

For younger students, this exercise may be completed verbally.

20. 60-SECOND RECALL

☆ **CATEGORY:** daily or single lesson closure activity   ☆ **AGES:** 7 and up

☆ **TIME:** 5–15 minutes

☆ **MATERIALS:** paper and pens or pencils (optional)

☆ **PURPOSE:** reinforce new skill(s) or information, address student questions and concerns, create personal meaning to improve student retention of new information and/or skills

PROCEDURE

Step 1. Demonstrate the start and stop signals to be used for this activity.

Step 2. When the start signal is given, students have 60 seconds to write down everything they remember about the lesson (or the whole day's lessons). Give the stop signal when time is up.

Step 3. Ask for volunteers (or randomly select students) to share what they wrote *(or try Step 4, next, for verbal responses instead of written ones).*

Step 4. If you prefer busy, active classrooms you can cue all students to talk at the same time while you roam the room and listen in. If you prefer quieter, calmer classrooms, you can designate 60 seconds of silent thinking and then ask for volunteers to share their answers verbally.

VARIATION

This activity can be done as a pair share—ask students to take turns telling their partners everything they remember from the lesson(s).

60-SECOND RECALL

226

Chapter Sixteen

Recapping the Course: End-of-Term Closure

It may be tempting to simply pack up the grade books and go (many college and university instructors skip the final class session and simply post grades outside their office doors), but this approach may leave some students—even adult students—feeling that their educational experience isn't quite complete.

People need to process the information and skills they have learned and the ideas that have been presented, especially if those ideas and skills were completely new ones or if they conflict with previously learned information and skills.

End-of-course closure activities can provide emotional and psychological closure for students, summarize key ideas from a course, acknowledge achievement, foster a sense of accomplishment, stimulate future learning, reinforce teacher-student bonds, and create an ongoing sense of community among students. My high school and college students frequently suggest passing around an optional sign-up sheet where students can list their phone numbers and e-mail addresses to be shared for future reference. Providing an opportunity for such sharing can be very helpful to students who are engaged in a specific course of study where a support network of colleagues can be very helpful to them in the future. These voluntary contact lists may also be helpful to younger learners who may want to locate homework and study partners.

Crossing Bridges

The twenty end-of-term closure activities outlined here are similar to daily closure activities but with a broader view, because of the multiple lessons, exercises, projects, and skills acquisition that a multiday or multiweek course encompasses. The focus here is different from the daily closure purpose. Instead of creating a bridge to the next day or the next class meeting, end-of-course activities allow students to take a look back at all the bridges they have crossed, reflect upon their own learning experiences, and mentally say goodbye.

Because time pressure is usually not such an issue at the end of a school term, and because students who know each other are often more inclined to actively participate than students who are strangers, end-of-course closure activities often take twenty or thirty minutes or more to complete, depending on the number, age, and personalities of students and the complexity of course content. If your final exam schedule allows time only for a brief closure activity, pencil it in on behalf of your students. Even a few minutes will be time well spent.

21. COUNTDOWN: 5, 4, 3, 2, 1

☆ **CATEGORY:** end-of-course closure activity ☆ **AGES:** 7 and up

☆ **TIME:** 5-15 minutes

☆ **MATERIALS:** chalkboard, whiteboard, or dry-erase board; or template handouts for students

☆ **PURPOSE:** reinforce learning, create personal connections to learning, provide student feedback and course closure

PROCEDURE

Step 1. Write a prompt on the board (or provide a paper template for students to use) that includes five numbered items:

5 things I learned in this class

4 ways this information or these skills will help me

3 ideas that occurred to me during this class

2 things I enjoyed doing in this class

1 thing I still want to know or that I would change about this class

Step 2. Ask students to share their responses with the class or form small groups and share with their groups. After 5-10 minutes, shuffle the group members so students share with different classmates.

VARIATIONS

This activity can be done as a whole class while you are writing down student responses on the board.

Students can write their own responses.

22. CLASS PORTRAIT

☆ **CATEGORY**: end-of-course closure activity   ☆ **AGES**: 7 and up

☆ **TIME**: 5–15 minutes

☆ **MATERIALS**: paper; crayons, markers, or colored pencils; digital camera

☆ **PURPOSE**: provide creative outlet and emotional release, reinforce learning, foster classroom community and student bonding, provide closure

PROCEDURE

Step 1. Distribute card stock, paper, or recycled paper (cardboard, paper bags, or paper that's been used on one side) and crayons, pencils, or markers.

Step 2. Display your own self-portrait as a model. (If you suspect that students may be insecure about their artistic abilities, you can intentionally draw a caricature or stick-figure self-portrait.)

Step 3. Students take 10–15 minutes to draw their own self-portraits and write the most important thing they have learned during the course.

Step 4. As students finish their portraits, they tack or tape them to the wall or bulletin board and admire their class portrait.

Step 5. If time permits and if students feel comfortable, you may ask each student to share his or her own most important knowledge.

Step 6. After all the portraits are posted, take a photo of them together as a class portrait. If the classroom has a computer with scanning capability, scan in the photo and print out copies for each student. If a scanner isn't available, take the photo and send it to students by e-mail or postal mail later.

VARIATIONS

If students will be working together in the future, you can allow a few minutes for them to circulate and exchange e-mail addresses by writing on the back of the portraits for future reference.

Instead of tacking portraits to the wall or bulletin board, you can ask students to stand, holding their portraits in front of their faces, for a group photo.

(continued)

CLASS PORTRAIT

Sample Class Portrait

23. CREATE A QUIZ

☆ *CATEGORY*: end-of-course closure activity   ☆ *AGES*: 7 and up

☆ *TIME*: 5–15 minutes

☆ *MATERIALS*: paper, pens or pencils

☆ *PURPOSE*: reinforce learning, create personal connections to learning, address student questions and concerns about course information, provide closure

PROCEDURE

Step 1. Give each student one or two slips of paper.

Step 2. Ask students to write quiz-style questions about the course.

Step 3. Collect all the questions and use them to create the final quiz, which can be given immediately or at the following class meeting. If the quiz is to be completed at the next meeting, you can opt to read out some or all of the questions to aid students in choosing what to study and review.

Step 4. Students complete the quiz and then work in pairs or small groups to discuss their answers and clarify any areas of confusion.

VARIATION

Instead of creating a final quiz, you can review the questions and use them to create an oral quiz or discussion on the same day that students create their questions.

24. DEAR ME

☆ **CATEGORY:** end-of-course closure activity   ☆ **AGES:** 7 and up

☆ **TIME:** 10–20 minutes

☆ **MATERIALS:** paper, pens or pencils, story or fable

☆ **PURPOSE:** reinforce learning, encourage student self-reflection, create personal connections to learning, provide student feedback and closure

PROCEDURE

Step 1. Find (or write) a fable, story, or book where one of the characters offers a different perspective on a familiar topic. For example, *The True Story of the Three Little Pigs*, by A. Wolf (Puffin, 1996), tells the story from the wolf's perspective and he proclaims his innocence.

Step 2. Read the selected story aloud to the class.

Step 3. Students write letters to themselves from the teacher, discussing their performance and behavior during the course. Some students will require starters for this exercise. Teachers may offer suggested beginnings such as the following four:

Dear Sally,

   It has been such a pleasure having you in my class because . . .

Dear Samantha,

   Wake up and smell the coffee! During this class . . .

Yo! Dude!

   Did you think I didn't notice all those times you were sleeping in class?

Dear David,

   Your parents would be so proud to know . . .

Step 4. Collect the letters to review later or, if appropriate for the group, read some letters aloud without revealing the authors' names.

VARIATIONS

Instead of reading the story aloud yourself, ask students to form small groups and select one member to read the story aloud before writing their individual letters.

Optional addition to this assignment: Ask students to include in their letters some mention of the grade the student should earn for the course and why.

Note: Although the book in this lesson starter was written for children, high school and adult students still respond enthusiastically to the exercise.

25. DEAR FUTURE STUDENT (OR DEAR NEW KID)

⭐ **CATEGORY:** end-of-course closure activity ⭐ **AGES:** 7 and up

⭐ **TIME:** 10–20 minutes

⭐ **MATERIALS:** paper, pens or pencils

⭐ **PURPOSE:** reinforce learning, encourage student self-reflection, create personal connections to learning, provide closure

PROCEDURE

Step 1. Provide paper or template for students to use. Provide written assignment sheet or visual display of directions on board or projector screen.

Step 2. Students write letters to future students (or new kids who will be taking the class), offering them specific suggestions and study tips for successfully completing the course.

Step 3. Collect the student advice letters to review, post them on the board for others to read, or allow students to share their letters in pairs or small groups.

VARIATION

If computers are available to students, they may opt to type and save or print their completed advice letters.

26. DIGITAL SCRAPBOOK

☆ **CATEGORY:** end-of-course closure activity   ☆ **AGES:** 7 and up

☆ **TIME:** 5–15 minutes

☆ **MATERIALS:** computer, scanner, digital camera

☆ **PURPOSE:** reinforce learning, encourage student self-reflection, create personal connections to learning, foster classroom community and student bonding, provide closure

PROCEDURE

Step 1. Invite students to create or find photos, drawings, websites, magazine articles, newspaper headlines, posters, and other materials that directly relate to the course topic.

Step 2. Take photos of students working together in the classroom and sharing the materials they brought.

Step 3. Scan the student materials and download the photos of students into the computer.

Step 4. Ask students to use the scanned images and photos to create a slideshow to be presented on the last day of class.

Step 5. Allow students to bring storage devices so they can make copies of the slideshow to take it home. Or post the slideshow on a website where students can access it.

VARIATION

Instead of a single slideshow, assign students to work in teams, with each team creating and presenting its own slideshow.

27. DRAW & DISCUSS

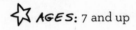 **CATEGORY:** end-of-course closure activity   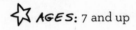 **AGES:** 7 and up

 TIME: 10–20 minutes

 MATERIALS: paper, pens, pencils, and/or markers

 PURPOSE: reinforce learning, encourage student self-reflection, create personal connections to learning, provide closure

PROCEDURE

Step 1. Ask each student to draw a picture, design, chart, or some other graphic representation of something they learned during the course.

Step 2. Display student drawings without explaining what they represent.

Step 3. Discuss drawings one at a time and see if classmates can correctly interpret each drawing. After classmates respond, ask the creator of the drawing to explain it.

VARIATION

If this activity is too abstract for your students, you might assign a specific topic from the course for them to illustrate, and then they can compare their illustrations. For example, you might ask them to create a flowchart showing a specific process or procedure or how to play a certain sport. Or ask them to create something that represents democracy or learning how to read.

28. FAMOUS QUOTATIONS

★ **CATEGORY:** end-of-course closure activity   ★ **AGES:** 7 and up

★ **TIME:** 5–15 minutes

★ **MATERIALS:** paper, pens or pencils; or poster board, markers; or computers

★ **PURPOSE:** review learning, encourage student self-reflection, create personal connections to learning, provide closure

PROCEDURE

Step 1. Locate a number of famous (or not-so-famous) quotations that relate to the topic of the course.

Step 2. Create a visual aid that displays the quotations and share it with students— for example, a poster, a slideshow, or a handout.

Step 3. Ask students to share their responses to the quotations in a whole-class or small-group discussion.

Step 4. Ask students to create their own "famous quotations" about the course and their recent learning.

Step 5. Ask students to copy their quotations, with or without illustrations, onto copier paper or poster board, or to create a digital slide for each quotation.

Step 6. Ask students to share and discuss their quotations.

VARIATIONS

If time permits, have students create a slideshow that includes all the quotations. Or have them make a brochure or printable handout of the quotations so all students can have a copy to take home.

For a more involved project, have students illustrate each quotation and create a children's-style picture book, with one quotation per page. If the book is created by hand, make a master copy that students can reproduce. If the book is created on the computer, make a PDF copy so the document can be shared across different networks.

29. I'M THE EXPERT

☆ **CATEGORY:** end-of-course closure activity   ☆ **AGES:** 7 and up

☆ **TIME:** varies depending on number and age of students

☆ **MATERIALS:** individually determined by students

☆ **PURPOSE:** reinforce learning, encourage student self-reflection, create personal connections to learning, provide closure

PROCEDURE

Step 1. Assign each student (or pairs or teams of students) the task of creating and performing a 5–10-minute demonstration of something they learned during the course.

Step 2. Encourage students to use visual aids, manipulatives, video, computers, and other objects to support their demonstrations.

Step 3. Take turns giving demonstrations and offer peer feedback (making sure to accentuate the positive).

VARIATION

To expand the possibilities, do not limit student demonstrations to course-related topics. Allow them to share other talents and skills such as juggling, cooking, martial arts, or woodworking—skills that are not normally involved in or recognized by the educational system.

30. I USED TO THINK

☆ **CATEGORY:** end-of-course closure activity ☆ **AGES:** 7 and up

☆ **TIME:** 5–15 minutes

☆ **MATERIALS:** (Optional) paper, pens or pencils; or butcher paper, markers

☆ **PURPOSE:** reinforce learning, encourage student self-reflection, create personal connections to learning, provide closure

PROCEDURE

Step 1. On the board, on a slide to be projected, or on a handout to be given to students, write the following prompt: "I used to think . . . but now I know . . ."

Step 2. Each student writes his or her response, completing the sentence.

Step 3. Students post their completed statements on the bulletin board or wall and browse, reading the different responses. (Some teachers simply let students complete the sentence in the prompt, then leave the completed responses on their desktops as they circulate through the room, reading each other's statements and discussing them informally.)

Step 4 (optional). Invite each student to explain and elaborate on his or her response to the prompt.

VARIATIONS

Instead of having students write their answers to the prompt, invite them to take turns responding verbally as individuals.

Assign students to work in pairs or teams and revise the prompt to read "*We* used to think . . ." Take turns sharing responses.

31 LEARNING TIPS

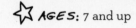

☆ *CATEGORY*: end-of-course closure activity   ☆ *AGES*: 7 and up

☆ *TIME*: 5–15 minutes

☆ *MATERIALS*: paper, pens or pencils, markers, computer, scanner (optional)

☆ *PURPOSE*: reinforce learning, encourage student self-reflection, create personal connections to learning, promote student interaction and bonding, provide closure

PROCEDURE

Step 1. Assign students to work in pairs or small groups.

Step 2. Instruct each team to design and create a one-page handout for future students that summarizes the key points of the course.

Step 3. Invite each team to present its handout to the class. Discuss and give feedback.

Step 4 (optional). If time and equipment permit, have students gather all the handouts and reproduce them as a booklet, adding illustrated front and back covers.

Step 5 (optional). Scan the handouts into a computer and create a slideshow or PDF document that can be e-mailed to students or placed on a public website.

VARIATION

Assign each team a different topic from the course, so that each handout covers different information.

32. PAPER QUILT

⭐ **CATEGORY:** end-of-course closure activity   ⭐ **AGES:** 6 and up

⭐ **TIME:** 10–25 minutes

⭐ **MATERIALS:** heavyweight paper, markers, single-hole punch, tape, yarn or twine

⭐ **PURPOSE:** reinforce learning, encourage student self-reflection, create personal connections to learning, promote student interaction and bonding, provide closure

PROCEDURE

Step 1. Precut squares of heavyweight paper or card stock to make enough for every student on your roster.

Step 2. Apply a small piece of tape to each corner of each square to prevent tearing (or purchase premade hole reinforcers). Punch a hole in each corner of each square.

Step 3. Precut yarn or twine into 6-inch lengths to make two pieces per student, along with a few spare pieces.

Step 4. Distribute paper squares and give students 5–10 minutes to decorate them and write one important thing or skill they learned during the course.

Step 5. Using the precut yard, attach the squares to each other to form a paper quilt that can be displayed on the wall. Thread and tie yarn through the unused holes to create a more finished look for the quilt.

VARIATION

Do this activity on the first day of class, with students decorating their squares to represent themselves and their interests, then repeat it periodically during the school year after you've completed major units of study to eventually form a final quilt to finish the year.

33. SCRAPBOOK

☆ **CATEGORY:** end-of-course closure activity   ☆ **AGES:** 7 and up

☆ **TIME:** 10–25 minutes (2-day activity)

☆ **MATERIALS:** heavyweight paper, pens, markers, glue, magazines, newspapers, digital camera

☆ **PURPOSE:** reinforce learning, encourage student self-reflection, promote classroom community and student bonding, create personal connections to learning, provide closure

PROCEDURE

Step 1. *Day one:* ask students to bring in photos, drawings, and print materials that pertain to the information and skills they learned during the course or year.

Step 2. *Day two:* distribute heavyweight paper to students, one sheet per student. (Keep a few spare sheets in case people "mess up" and need to start over.) Provide old newspapers and magazines to cut up and use, as well as markers and glue.

Step 3. Give students a specified time period in which to create their individual learning pages.

Step 4 *(optional).* While students are working, take photos of them to be included in the teacher's page of the scrapbook, along with a photo of you. A class photo may also be taken by somebody from outside the class.

Step 5. Collect the individual pages and bind them with yarn, staples, or glue to create a class scrapbook.

Step 6. Write the date and have all students (and the teacher) autograph the first page of the scrapbook, adding any individual comments they may choose.

Step 7. Select volunteers or work as a class to design and create the back and front covers to the scrapbook.

Step 8. Store or display the scrapbook for future visits from former students.

34. SELF-ASSESSMENT

☆ **CATEGORY:** end-of-course closure activity   ☆ **AGES:** 7 and up

☆ **TIME:** 5–20 minutes

☆ **MATERIALS:** paper, pens; or template

☆ **PURPOSE:** reinforce learning, encourage student self-reflection, create personal connections to learning, provide closure

PROCEDURE

Step 1. On the board or on a slide that is projected onto a screen, display the assignment instructions. Or provide a template to hand out to students with blanks for the student's name, date, course name or number, and suggested final grade, followed by blank lines for students to write their justification for the final grade they would give themselves in this course.

Step 2. Give students a specified time period to write a brief self-assessment of themselves as learners in this specific course, critiquing their own attendance, behavior, participation, effort, and grades earned on various assignments.

Step 3 *(optional).* Hold a brief personal conference with each student at the teacher's desk or in a corner of the classroom to discuss their self-assessments and offer feedback and suggestions to help the students enjoy continued success in their future studies. These conferences can take place during the final exam period, if appropriate.

Step 4. Collect the self-assessments for use during final grade computation. If time permits and if returning the assessments is appropriate, provide written feedback on the assessments and return them to students after final grades have been posted.

VARIATIONS

This activity can be used at the end of a unit of study or as a midterm assessment so that you can offer suggestions and guidance over the course of the school term.

Adapt this activity as a precourse assessment by eliminating the reference to final grades and instead asking students to assess themselves as learners in your subject area.

35. SIX-WORD MEMOIRS

☆ **CATEGORY:** end-of-course closure activity ☆ **AGES:** 7 and up

☆ **TIME:** 5–15 minutes

☆ **MATERIALS:** paper; pens, pencils, and/or markers

☆ **PURPOSE:** reinforce learning, encourage student self-reflection, create personal connection to learning, promote student discussion, provide closure

PROCEDURE

Step 1. Visit the National Public Radio website to view a gallery of illustrated 6-word memoirs that were part of a project for *Smith* magazine, in which writers were asked to distill their lives to six words: www.npr.org/templates/story/story.php?storyId=18768430. The project led to the book *Not Quite What I Was Planning* (HarperPerennial, 2008).

Step 2. Create two or three sample 6-word memoirs that represent fictional students who have studied your particular course or subject(s).

Step 3. Give students a specified time period in which to create their own 6-word memoirs about themselves as students in your class (or as students in general). Some students enjoy decorating or illustrating their memoirs; others prefer to use words alone.

Step 4. Ask students to post their completed memoirs on a bulletin board or wall so classmates can browse and discuss them. Or ask each student to present his or her memoir to the class.

VARIATIONS

Scan the memoirs into the computer and create a slideshow for students to watch and discuss. Or, if computers are available to students, allow them to create the memoirs on the computer and assign them to work in teams to create team slideshows to share with the class.

Note: This activity is similar to Six-Word Summaries in Chapter Eight. The two activities create excellent beginning and ending brackets for a course. If you save the summaries from the first activity, you can post them alongside the memoirs.

(continued)

(continued)

Sometimes, Students Are My Best Teachers!

A+ A+ A+ A+

Teachers who LISTEN hear more learning

A Teacher is an open book

Fired UP's and 's and Ready to Teach

Sample Six-Word Memoirs

36 STORY TIME

☆ **CATEGORY:** end-of-course closure activity ☆ **AGES:** 6 and up
☆ **TIME:** 5–15 minutes
☆ **MATERIALS:** course-related story, fable, parable, or myth
☆ **PURPOSE:** reinforce learning, create personal connection to learning, encourage student self-reflection, promote student discussion, provide closure

PROCEDURE

Step 1. Find or write a short fable, story, myth, or parable that relates to the course or subject of study. A quick online search will locate many possibilities. School librarians are also a good resource.

Step 2. If possible, print and distribute copies of the reading, so students who are not auditory processors can follow along.

Step 3. Invite students to share their responses to the reading as a whole class or in small groups or pairs.

Step 4 (optional). If time permits, ask students to draw or write a response to the reading, or to write their own myth, fable or parable to share with the class.

VARIATION

Find or create an audio recording (or video) of an appropriate story or excerpt from a longer work. Make a copy of the reading and play the recording as students follow along.

37. TWENTY QUESTIONS

☆ **CATEGORY**: end-of-course closure activity   ☆ **AGES**: 7 and up

☆ **TIME**: 20–30 minutes (one or two class periods)

☆ **MATERIALS**: paper, pens or pencils

☆ **PURPOSE**: reinforce learning, create personal connection to learning, promote student discussion and interaction, provide closure

PROCEDURE

Step 1. Assign students to work in small groups or pairs.

Step 2. Give teams a specific time period in which to write twenty questions about information and skills studied during the course.

Step 3. Collect questions and randomly redistribute them to teams, making sure that no team receives its own questions.

Step 4. Give teams a specific time period to see how many questions they can answer correctly.

Step 5. Discuss any particular areas of misunderstanding or confusion as a class.

VARIATIONS

Younger students can be asked to write ten questions instead of twenty.

If appropriate, have students write their questions during one class period, then trade questions and work on answers during the subsequent class meeting.

38. WHO WANTS TO EARN AN A?

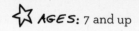

☆ **CATEGORY:** end-of-course closure activity   ☆ **AGES:** 7 and up

☆ **TIME:** 15–30 minutes

☆ **MATERIALS:** projector and screen

☆ **PURPOSE:** reinforce learning, create personal connection to learning, provide closure

PROCEDURE

Step 1. Create a list of multiple-choice and short-answer questions based on key concepts, information, and skills learned during the course.

Step 2. Make a slide for each question that can be projected using an overhead projector, LCD projector, or interactive whiteboard. Use a large enough font so slides can be easily read from the back of the classroom.

Step 3. Using the format of the TV program *Who Wants to Be a Millionaire?* decide how many questions students will have to answer in order to earn an A. Ten is a good number for older students, five for younger students.

Step 4. Create a template that can be used to tally student scores (or keep a tally on a whiteboard or presentation easel). Show a pyramid or some other graphic to depict the number of questions that must be answered correctly in order to win.

Step 5. Decide whether contestants will be allowed to ask a friend, consult the audience, or check the text one time during their attempt to reach the A.

Step 6. Place a chair facing away from the class for the contestant to sit in while answering questions. Select contestants via a random drawing. For larger classes, you may opt to select pairs or teams to work together as contestants.

Step 7. Before beginning the game, explain to the audience that no talking will be allowed during the time when a question is asked and the contestant responds. Noncontestants are invited to take notes during the game to use as a study guide.

VARIATION

This is a popular activity and can be used throughout the term as a review for exams and quizzes.

Note: I have actually used this activity as a genuine challenge for high school students, using challenging and complex questions from the final exam. If students reached the A without being disqualified, they earned an A on their final exam. To make sure the A contestants had truly earned their As, any time a student won the game, they also took the final exam. No winner has ever failed to earn an A on the actual exam.

39. WORDS OF WISDOM

☆ **CATEGORY:** end-of-course closure activity ☆ **AGES:** 7 and up

☆ **TIME:** 10–20 minutes

☆ **MATERIALS:** none required

☆ **PURPOSE:** reinforce learning, create personal connection to learning, promote student discussion and interaction, provide closure

PROCEDURE

Step 1. Place student chairs or desks in a circle or semicircle. If the room is too small to rearrange furniture, ask students to stand or find a location outside of the classroom.

Step 2. Ask students to think silently about their experience in the class—how the class has affected them, what they have learned, and what they would still like to learn.

Step 3. Invite students to step forward one at a time and take 60 seconds to say whatever they would like to share about their experience in the class without being interrupted by anybody. Provide a timer so students will know when their time is up.

Step 4 *(optional).* After each student takes a turn, give the class 60 seconds to respond. When the time is up, don't delay—move to the next person.

VARIATION

Invite students to take turns asking questions of the teacher.

40. WRITE A BOOK

☆ **CATEGORY:** end-of-course closure activity   ☆ **AGES:** 7 and up

☆ **TIME:** 20–45 minutes or longer

☆ **MATERIALS:** paper, markers; or computers with word-processing software

☆ **PURPOSE:** reinforce learning, create personal connection to learning, promote student discussion and interaction, provide closure

PROCEDURE

Step 1. Assign students to work in pairs or teams.

Step 2. Give students a specific time period to write and illustrate a children's picture book on a key topic from the course. You may elect to assign topics to avoid repetition or you may allow students to choose their own topics with teacher approval.

Step 3. Save each book as a PDF document that can be stored on a public website or sent to students via e-mail. (If books are created on paper, scan them into the computer and convert them to PDF docs.)

Step 4 (optional). Print out copies of books for students.

Step 5. Invite each team to present and read its book to the class. Provide peer critiques and feedback.

Step 6. Make a copy of the book to be placed in the school library. Include a page listing the date the book was created and include the authors' names.

Step 7 (optional). Invite parents and/or other classes to attend a public reading of the books. Film the reading, if possible. (Teams who are too shy to read their books aloud can ask a classmate to read their books for them.)

VARIATION

This exercise can be used effectively as a review at the end of a unit of study. One biology teacher I know assigned this as a project after the class had studied the cell. Some of the books her students created were good enough to be submitted to publishers. And students who participated in the project also earned excellent scores on the exam for the unit.

WRITE A BOOK

Appendix

We Want More!

A quick search for 'classroom icebreakers' on the Internet will yield dozens of sources. (If you search for just the word <u>icebreakers</u> you may find yourself reading articles about methods of breaking ice from the hulls of ships sailing in chilly waters.)

The following is just a handful of the good sites from a recent online search for web pages that do not require visitors to register or sign up in order to access free information. Each of these links will lead you to more free resources.

→ *http://adulted.about.com/od/icebreakers*
   Includes icebreakers designed specially for adults and links to team-building games.

→ *http://pbskids.org/zoom/activities/sci*
   Science activities listed by category, such as chemistry, engineering, structures, forces, life science, sound, and water.

→ www.archimedes-lab.org/droodles.html
   Website with samples and links to more "droodles" (word pictures
   popularized by cartoonist Roger Price in the 1950s). A droodle is a cross
   between a doodle and a riddle, and there is no single correct answer.
   According to this website, droodles are based on the human tendency to
   impose a pattern on, or find meaning in, random or ambiguous shapes.

→ www.educationworld.com
   Search for "icebreakers" to find a number of links, as well as lessons,
   professional development resources, and technology integration information.

→ www.dr-mikes-math-games-for-kids.com/index.html
   A good selection of math games divided by grade level.

→ www.education-world.com/a_lesson/lesson074.shtml
   Search for "icebreakers" on this site to find a number of links, as well as
   lessons, professional development resources, information for administrators,
   and technology integration.

→ www.esl4teachers.com/icebreakers.php
   Lesson plans, templates, rubrics, and worksheets.

→ www.icebreakergames.co.uk
   Website exclusively dedicated to collecting successful icebreakers. Has
   articles supporting use of icebreakers, advice, and guidelines for using them
   effectively and avoiding time-wasters. Under the Education link, you will find
   icebreakers specifically designed for adults, first days of school, non-English
   speakers, primary school students, children with learning disabilities, adult
   students, and international students.

→ www.icebreakers.ws
   Good selection of icebreakers and team-building activities.

→ http://www.kimskorner4teachertalk.com/classmanagement/icebreakers.html
   Super selection of icebreakers and energizers from a teacher with over
   sixteen years of experience teaching language arts and ESL. Many more links
   on this great site.

➔ *www.lessonplanspage.com/BeginSchool.htm*
Dozens of icebreakers are listed by category, such as art, computers, language arts, math, music, and physical education.

➔ *http://www.scholastic.com/teachers*
Check this site for a variety of daily starting activities designed to suit various grade levels.

➔ *www.virginia.edu/french/resource/teachers/tips/picture.htm*
Detailed instructions for using icebreakers with pictures for students of French. Can be adapted for other languages.

➔ *www.worksheetlibrary.com/teachingtips/icebreakers.html*
Find free lesson plans divided by grade level, subject, and standards.

INDEX

C

D

E

F

Y